# Working Together

# Reading and Writing in Inclusive Classrooms

Marilyn C. Scala
Port Washington, New York, USA

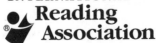

INTERNATIONAL
Reading
Association

800 Barksdale Road, PO Box 8139
Newark, Delaware 19714-8139, USA
www.reading.org

The International Reading Association attempts, through its publications, to provide a forum for a wide spectrum of opinions on reading. This policy permits divergent viewpoints without implying the endorsement of the Association.

**Director of Publications**   Joan M. Irwin
**Editorial Director, Books and Special Projects**   Matthew W. Baker
**Senior Editor, Books and Special Projects**   Tori Mello Bachman
**Permissions Editor**   Janet S. Parrack
**Production Editor**   Shannon Benner
**Assistant Editor**   Corinne M. Mooney
**Editorial Assistant**   Tyanna L. Collins
**Publications Manager**   Beth Doughty
**Production Department Manager**   Iona Sauscermen
**Supervisor, Electronic Publishing**   Anette Schütz-Ruff
**Senior Electronic Publishing Specialist**   Cheryl J. Strum
**Electronic Publishing Specialist**   R. Lynn Harrison
**Proofreader**   Charlene M. Nichols

**Project Editors**   Matthew W. Baker and Shannon Benner

**Cover Design and Illustration**   Pneuma Books: Complete Publisher's Services

**Library of Congress Cataloging in Publication Data**
Scala, Marilyn C., 1942–
    Working together : reading and writing in inclusive classrooms /
Marilyn C. Scala.
        p.   cm.
Includes bibliographical references and index.
    ISBN 0-87207-298-3
1. Special education—United States.   2. Language arts (Elementary)—United States.
3. Reading—Remedial teaching—United States.   4. Inclusive education—United
States.   5. Group work in education—United States.   I. Title.
    LC3973 .S32 2001
    371.9'046—dc21

                                                                              2001004905

# Contents

# Preface

### The Clay Falcon

*The falcon burst*
*out of the clay*
*like a bull bursting*
*out of a wall.*

*I stared*
*wondering what kind of falcon*
*it was.*
*It looked at me*
*and its eyes*
*shone sky blue.*

*My heart went fast*
*as*
*its wings reached out*
*to the sky*
*and it took off.*

*Light shone through*
*her wings.*
*She climbed the sky*
*as if the wind*
*were a ladder.*

*I ran just in time*
*to see her swoop up*
*and down into*
*heaven.*

*Then I stopped*
*to see her*
*disappear.*

*I fell.*
*I wanted to cry*
*because it felt good*
*to let such beauty*
*free.*

*My eyes drop*
*one tear*
*on each eye.*

This poem was written by Jamar, a student who received special education services. When he wrote the poem, Jamar was in an inclusive fifth-grade classroom. With his classmates, he learned about birds of prey and dissected owl pellets. With assistance from me and another classmate, he read the novel *My Side of the Mountain* by Jean Craighead George (2000).

Students with disabilities benefit from reading and writing in general education classrooms where literacy is a personal, academic, and social event in which children are immersed all day. In the inclusive classrooms where I worked first as a special education teacher and now as a consultant for literacy and inclusion, students are listening, speaking, reading, and writing across curriculum areas using fiction, nonfiction, and poetry. The teachers model learning strategies and guide students toward increasing independence. Instruction in reading includes reading in social studies and science as well as literature and personal choice. Reading is connected to writing and discussion, which enhances reading comprehension and retention for all students. Students with disabilities will miss these activities, spread throughout the day, if we isolate them to remediate their deficits in an attempt to bring them to grade level before they join their peers.

*Working Together: Reading and Writing in Inclusive Classrooms* is a book about meeting the needs of *all* students—especially those in the intermediate grades with mild to moderate disabilities who need special education services—by teaching them in inclusive classrooms. Throughout the book, you will meet children with special needs who are developing skills, motivation, and self-esteem in the rich language environments of general education classrooms. You will also meet their teachers, who are working through continual reflection and problem solving as they discover the educational philosophies, classroom structures, and learning strategies that lead to students' success.

*Working Together* is organized into chapters according to the components of a balanced approach to literacy instruction:

- *Read-alouds.* During read-alouds, children learn by listening. Too often, readers with disabilities tend to associate reading with struggling. Reading to students helps them associate reading with pleasure and familiarizes them with different types of literature and authors. Students connect to the books during oral conversations and often write entries in their writer's notebooks.

- *Independent reading and writing.* Allotting time for practicing reading and writing skills independently is essential. Again, struggling readers may tend to avoid books altogether. Students should have time in school to read books of choice at their comfortable reading level, and to write on topics of choice. We need to help them find material they can enjoy, and we need to make reading and writing important in and out of school.

- *Shared reading and writing.* During shared reading and writing activities, children learn from modeling and demonstration. This is an interactive period in which teachers and students explore a variety of texts for specific purposes. It differs from read-alouds in that students see the text, and teachers stop frequently during the reading to interact with students and facilitate their use of strategies. As students with disabilities see their nondisabled peers take risks with learning and make mistakes, they perceive approximations as part of the learning process, not as something that happens only to them.

- *Guided reading and writing.* This involves practicing new skills with guidance. It is the time in the reading-writing workshop when teachers work with individual students or with small groups of students on an instructional level. Teachers develop lessons with a particular focus to scaffold students to the next level of competence, encouraging them to set goals and monitor their own progress. Again, this practice reminds children with disabilities that *all* students benefit from guidance, not just poor readers.

Inclusion in this book also occurs through collaborative learning and co-teaching. Although there is no one right way to implement inclusion in our schools, the collaboration of students working in heterogeneous groups with general education teachers and special education teachers who plan, co-teach, and evaluate together is key to its success.

Collaboration and cooperation are necessary skills for the classroom, the workplace, and life. By working together, students and teachers learn to set group goals, and they learn about cooperative decision making and problem solving. As I have worked with other teachers in inclusive classrooms, we have discovered that when two teachers are present and the students work in large or small groups, the children

- have better retention and higher achievement,
- receive more individual attention,
- show greater intrinsic motivation,
- develop more positive attitudes and relationships,
- evidence higher self-esteem based on self-acceptance, and
- show greater ability to view situations from others' perspectives.

Jamar's poem about letting a falcon fly free is an ideal message to open this book, because you will soon see how reading and writing in inclusive classrooms can bring students with disabilities and in general education their own sense of freedom.

*MCS*

# Acknowledgments

I will be forever grateful for all the children I work with now and have worked with over the years, for they always show me the way to new thinking. I must thank my friends and mentors who propel me into exciting new ways of teaching and continually inform my beliefs—Bee Cullinan for listening to my stories about children and encouraging me to write; Ralph Fletcher and his writing workshops, which changed both me and my students; Diane Snowball and her way of looking at learners of all ages; Angela Jaggar, who was an invaluable resource; and Tom Seavey, who knew just what books would influence my professional growth. I am indebted to the members of my writing group—Bee Cullinan, Ginnie Schroder, Joie Hinden, Ann Lovett, and Debbie Wooten—who have read parts of this book over the last few years and have always been supportive. I must also thank my colleagues and friends in special education and general education for our work and conversations together, especially Sue Slavin and Rochelle Glick. For making this book possible and for their guidance and patience, I thank Joan Irwin, Matt Baker, Shannon Benner, and Renee Nicholls. Last, but most essential, is my love and thanks to my family, who have always believed in me and encouraged me through my years in the classroom and my hours at the computer.

CHAPTER

# 1

# Teaching in Inclusive Classrooms: A Beginning

I have not always worked in inclusive classrooms. For 20 years I was a special education teacher with a room of my own. The students in my first class had multiple handicaps, the most obvious being cerebral palsy. Some children communicated with a roll of the eye or by hitting a buzzer with a toe to answer yes or no. We studied in all academic areas, reading and writing about the same topics our general education peers were doing down the hall. We joined them for recess after lunch, but we did not team with other classes for science, social studies, or simply to enjoy a good book together.

My next assignment, teaching students with emotional and learning disabilities, was in a New York City school where special classes were in a wing by themselves. We were segregated from general education peers by location, lunch hour, and staff attitude. Although I tried to create materials that would be interesting to my students, I was trained in a diagnostic-prescriptive approach that relied more on building skills at the deficit level than on authentic and age-appropriate learning tasks.

When I moved to the suburbs, I taught first and second grade in general education classrooms. I shifted from a remedial framework to one that embraced the curriculum. I planned for the students who learned everything I taught in minutes and for those who needed review and repetition.

In 1975, I returned to special education when my district created programs for students with disabilities. The programs were a result of Public Law 94-142—now known as the Individuals with Disabilities Education Act (IDEA)—which was the first major educational restructuring in special education. This act guarantees free, appropriate public education for all children with disabilities. It requires that students with disabilities be educated with their nondisabled peers to the maximum extent possible—that is, in the least restrictive environment. In programs developed as a result of IDEA, an interdisciplinary team of teachers, parents, and administrators develops a written plan, known as an individualized educational program (IEP), that identifies a student's levels of performance and details the special education services he or she must receive. The IEP outlines the areas needing remediation through goals and objectives and specifies the time to be spent in special education and general education classrooms.

In the special education program in which I worked, students identified as having special needs were pulled out of their regular classes for part of the day. I worked with children for the time specified on each IEP. I chose the books to read, the curriculum to modify, and the remedial strategies to implement. I taught within this structure for 15 years, diagnosing, remediating, planning creative activities, and helping students with their work from general education classrooms. Like many special educators, I tried to connect the prescriptive remediation, which was deficit driven, with their regular class activities, which often included regular class assignments that needed completion or explanation. For the most part, the students were successful and their parents were happy. So why did I change? The changes occurring in language arts in general education classrooms caused me to revise my philosophy on how to best meet the needs of children with disabilities.

The 1980s and 1990s stand out as decades of educational restructuring in general education classrooms. School districts began implementing process writing, and students wrote daily—drafting, conferencing, revising, and editing before arriving at final copies that were "published." Many teachers abandoned basal readers and workbooks. They began to teach with articles and whole novels, facilitating group discussions and using authentic follow-up activities. The school environment changed from one in which the teacher imparted skills and information to one where teacher and students worked together as learners. The curriculum became child centered—not merely an accumulation of facts, but a process in which learners interact within a resource-rich environment to construct new meanings. I wanted to create the same process and environment in my pull-out program for students with disabilities.

Initially, I tried teaching with trade books and group discussions. One group consisted of 4 fifth-grade boys who were reading 2 years below grade level. Using whole books instead of basal excerpts, we read, wrote, listened to one another, and retold stories with our opinions. As a result, their social behaviors improved. They learned to accept praise comfortably, refrain from put-downs, and give positive feedback to one another. Furthermore, their academic behaviors also changed as they began to respond in various ways to literature and learn strategies for constructing meaning from the text. Kenny's and Joshua's writing began to show their critical thinking abilities, and James and Matt progressed from writing a short paragraph in their response journals to rambling on proudly for six pages or more, a marked improvement in time on task if not yet in full comprehension and higher level thinking. However, our pace was rather slow, and our models for reading and writing in this small special education group were confined to one teacher (me) or an assistant, and several reader-writers with disabilities.

Later that year, I asked Ann, a fifth-grade teacher, if a group of my students and I could join her class for book discussions. Part of the philosophy of a balanced literacy approach to learning is that it is implemented with heterogeneous groups of learners. I wondered how such class discussions would enrich my students' work habits and understanding of the literature.

Being included in the general education class improved my students' motivation and self-esteem. Armed with the security that my assistant or I would help them be prepared, they began to set new academic goals and reach them. Ann and I gave all the students a choice of novels on different reading levels, and we each worked with heterogeneous groups of students to prepare them for book discussions. Kenny, Joshua, James, and Matt, my first trial group of special education-inclusion students, became problem solvers, increasing their work pace and getting the work done with help at home, help in school (from teachers or nondisabled peers), and the use of some taped books. Kenny became less aloof, Joshua dropped his class clown behavior, and James and Matt gradually relinquished habits of dependence and avoidance.

Most important, these students with special needs learned that *all* children have questions and reread for understanding. After listening to the journal responses of their peers, they began to focus their responses on characters and issues. They began to see that ability might be less a factor in their final products than time on task, and that the strategies they were being encouraged to use were strategies that *all* good readers and writers use. The interaction with general education class peers, the general education class teacher, and the special education teacher forged a more powerful change in the students with disabilities, both academically and socially, than I was able to achieve in the pull-out model.

# What Is Inclusion?

What exactly is *inclusion*? Much is being written about it, and sometimes I think that inclusion has as many definitions as it has implementations. In the inclusion model described in this book, students benefit *academically and socially* from the activities in the general education classroom with the *support and collaboration* of the special education staff. Inclusion, in this text, is a classroom environment that incorporates the participation, friendship, and interaction of students with disabilities in general education settings. It does not mean the dismantling of the special education system and the return of all students to the general education classroom without academic support and benefit.

Inclusion is very different from pulling students out of the classroom for special education services and "mainstreaming" them for selected activities. With inclusion, special educators co-teach in general education classrooms, and all children see them as a resource. Productive learning communities are formed. In collaborative classrooms, special needs children are more motivated to use specific strategies when they see that these are the strategies all learners use. They respond to the respect and positive feedback they get from peers and teachers, and they set goals of their own. They become more assertive in problem solving and are able to seek help from several adults or peers. As student attitudes and behaviors change, they spend more time on task and achieve greater academic and social success.

## Cambourne's Theory of Literacy Learning

Brian Cambourne (1995) developed a theory of learning that he has since applied to literacy. He began his research because he was continually surprised and confused by students who did not seem able to learn simple reading, writing, and math concepts but could apply more complex knowledge and skills to solving problems in the everyday world. He wondered how a brain could master such complex learning outside school and be deficient in the kinds of learning needed inside school. His conditions of learning include the following:

- *Immersion.* Learners need to be immersed in text of all kinds.
- *Demonstration.* Learners need many demonstrations of how texts are constructed and used.
- *Expectations.* Learners are most likely to engage in demonstrations with those who hold high expectations of them.
- *Responsibility.* Learners need to be able to make some decisions as to the nature of the engagement that will occur.
- *Employment.* Learners need time and opportunity to practice their developing control in functional, relevant ways.
- *Approximations.* Learners must be free to approximate the desired model. "Mistakes" are essential for learning to occur.
- *Response.* Learners must receive feedback from more knowledgeable others that is relevant, timely, and nonthreatening.

Learner engagement is key. For active participation, there needs to be a perceived need and purpose for learning. Cambourne values learners' ability to express knowledge in their own words. Understanding is enhanced through discussion with others and an interchange of interpretations and understandings.

Cambourne's data show a strong relation among effective literacy learning and reflection, the development of conscious awareness of how language and learning work, and the evaluation of self. His theory is relevant for students with disabilities, who should perceive a need and purpose for learning, make some decisions as to the nature of their engagement, and have time to practice their developing control in functional, relevant ways.

# Literacy Learning for Students With Disabilities

In inclusive classrooms, students with disabilities learn with their peers and respond with the motivation that comes from being part of the intellectual and social mainstream. They are reading, writing, listening, and speaking to gain information, to construct meaning, to make connections between books and their own lives, and simply for pleasure. The general education teacher and special educator continually give support in the development of learning strategies as students read and write together from a variety of materials and for a variety of purposes.

Brianna is an example of what can happen in an inclusive environment. Before fourth grade, she was in a pull-out model for special education services. She was considerably behind her peers in academic work, and her impulsive and attention-getting behaviors interfered with her accomplishments, both in her special education and general education classrooms.

In fourth grade, she stayed in the general education class for the entire day. My assistant or I were in her classroom for 120 minutes a day, the period of time specified on her IEP. During this time, there was a balance of literacy activities taking place—some read-alouds, book discussions, time for independent reading, and a variety of lessons on strategies that good readers and writers need. Brianna discovered the joy of listening to taped books, which she understood well, so she was able to join class discussions. She was able to dictate some of the writing activities, and cooperative grouping allowed her to be a part of content area study.

In this inclusive setting, both Brianna's behavior and learning improved. The classroom teacher and I were pleased that her primary disability classification changed from ED (emotionally disturbed) to LD (learning disabled), and that she changed from feeling like an outsider to one who belonged in her classroom. Her academic and social progress were such that she even received an award from a local organization for improving her grades.

This progress in no way negated what the special education and general education teachers before fourth grade were offering in pull-out services. However, when Brianna was helped separately, she did not feel as capable as her peers, and she did not monitor her behavior as well either. At the end of her year in an inclusive classroom, she was able to dictate her reflection on reading for her portfolio. The following excerpt reveals how positive she felt about her growth:

> I feel like I accomplished my goals by listening to other people's responses and trying to make them as good as I can. The most important thing I like about reading is that

you learn new stuff. For fun I like to read the American Girl collection. The important thing about getting a good grade is listening and that's what I do. In the beginning of the year I used to stutter but now that I'm used to reading my responses in front of people, I say my response clear as the wind.

# Teacher Collaboration

In the inclusive classrooms in which I work, the special education teacher collaborates with general education teachers. We plan together, share successes, and brainstorm problems until we find solutions—together. Key to the success of inclusion is for general education teachers and special education teachers to co-teach. This differentiates inclusion from mainstreaming.

When writing an article for *Creative Classroom* (Scala, 1998), I asked teachers across the United States if inclusion was working in their schools. Although their school districts were implementing inclusion in a variety of ways, it became clear that inclusion was most successful when it was supported by teacher collaboration. Lisa, a general education teacher from Nebraska, felt the key was proper planning. She met with the special education teacher weekly to communicate ideas, plan, and prepare materials. She explained, "With two teachers, we are able to assist and monitor students so much more effectively."

Melina, a special educator from Pennsylvania, agreed that inclusion worked best when students had the support they needed while in the general education classroom. She noted, "Inclusion is an ongoing project that needs to be worked out on a daily basis…and as soon as the rough edges are smoothed out and there is support and cooperation between special and general educators, inclusion could become a way of life."

The professional growth that can take place between colleagues in inclusive classrooms is very powerful. I have always loved teaching, but I have learned more and had more fun since I began co-teaching with other teachers. In the district where I worked as a special education teacher for many years, some collaborations stand out as exceptional experiences for all who were involved:

The special education students in Tricia Ferraro's class needed support in writing skills, so our inclusion time was used primarily for writer's workshop. Many of the general education students in the class also had weak writing skills, so we collaborated daily on assignments such as student response to literature or writing to a prompt. In addition, we planned several genre studies in writing during the year. In each study, students worked for weeks reading and writing poetry, personal vignettes, and nonfiction. While students were researching for their nonfiction pieces, we analyzed feature articles and opinion pieces from student magazines. Students chose their topics of interest, reading and writing about subjects as diverse as skateboarding and the genetics of twins. Then they selected their format—a feature article or opinion piece. Tricia and I shared in preparing the minilessons needed, and we divided the class, each conferencing with half, during the research and writing processes. We communicated several times a week to plan and assess. It was a wonderful learning experience for the entire class, including the teachers.

Ginnie Schroder and I also began working as inclusion colleagues. Her class was already rich in literature and reading and writing connections to the curriculum. I brought strategies for comprehension and techniques for writing poetry. She planned her day so that there was a block of reading-writing time each afternoon for the 90 minutes I was in her room. This time was sometimes used for group lessons in which one of us would demonstrate a strategy for reading or do a minilesson on an aspect of writing. Sometimes we would list on the board the work in progress and let students choose what they needed most to do. This openness in the reading-writing literacy block enabled us to meet the needs of each child, whether we were working with groups or with an individual student. In addition, Ginnie and I often demonstrated strategies such as inference or theme using poetry. A few years after we started to co-teach with inclusion, we worked with Bernice Cullinan to coauthor *Three Voices: An Invitation to Poetry Across the Curriculum* (1995), and we are still collaborating as we now consult in schools doing literacy training.

Iris Gandler, a general education teacher, and I teamed for 2 hours a day for inclusion. We started the school year with read-alouds and journal entries. Later, we used most of our time together for shared or guided lessons. We teamed for minilessons, literature circles, and units of study in social studies and science. Our journal entries during read-alouds became the seeds for our writing workshops during the year. I led most of the writing workshop work; Iris led most of the study in the curriculum areas. I found the picture books to support our theme studies in science and social studies while Iris developed the rubrics and flowcharts on the computer that would support our long-range studies. Our different professional interests complemented each other.

My relationship with each teacher was different. To me, inclusion is to education as jazz is to music. A beginning listener might think that each jazz musician is just going off on his or her own, improvising as the mood fits. But a closer look reveals the musicians' respect for the music and for each other as they bring their individuality to the structure of the piece. As educators, we work within the structure of our philosophies, the curriculum, and students' needs. Then through conversation, planning, and creative improvisation, we find ways to create the jazz compositions in our field—successful students.

Of course, not every relationship plays like a piece of jazz. During the years I collaborated as a special education teacher in general education classrooms, some teachers were reluctant to give up a room of their own and share their classroom and students with me. One teacher wanted to assign me to the special education students and give me specific directions as to what she wanted done. Another teacher agreed to team for guided reading, then grouped the students without my input, placing all the special education students and the general education students with difficulties in my group. Another teacher welcomed the idea of collaborating and, once I arrived, left on extended coffee breaks.

I have seen situations in which the special education teachers go into the general education classrooms and sit only with the students with special needs. In these cases, the general education teachers feel like they are being observed and doing all the preparation for teaching, while the special education teachers feel like assistants and wonder when they will use all their training. When special education teachers work only with their students, the special education students feel different too.

What can be done when these situations happen? In my case, I had developed friendly relationships with these teachers over the years, but sharing a classroom is different than talking over lunch. I wanted to work out the problems in a comfortable and professional way, so I returned to the education theories that were encouraged in our school, such as the principles of heterogeneous grouping and conflict resolution.

In this way, our attempts to overcome the hurdles in the change to co-teaching became professional, not personal. We defined the problem in terms of students' needs instead of blame, brainstormed a number of possible solutions, decided on a mutually acceptable solution, and evaluated it, trying another if necessary. We looked at the students' IEPs to establish the areas in which we would team. We referred to the philosophies of a balanced literacy approach to help us plan what strategies to model for the whole class. Then we broke students into smaller groups at different levels to guide them in using the strategy, and to encourage them to practice independently. As time passed, we learned to become comfortable with each other's styles and to confirm that working together was collaborative, not evaluative. From difficult beginnings, our relationships as collaborators grew, and over the years we shared in many student successes.

## Student Classifications

The special education students I refer to in this book are students who have mild to moderate disabilities and are usually classified as learning disabled, emotionally disabled, speech and language disabled, and other health impaired. I have included these labels as a framework to show the types of children with whom I am working for the purpose of creating inclusive environments. At this time, the labels remain necessary to guarantee that students receive help and to enable teachers to have the support they need to ensure that every student is successful. However, as special education teachers begin to provide services in general education classrooms, I hope the need for labeling will decrease.

*Learning Disabilities.* Students with learning disabilities have significant difficulty in understanding or using spoken or written language. They may have short-term or long-term memory problems or difficulty with retrieval and transfer of information. Many have weak visual, auditory, motor, and/or organization skills. For students to be classified as learning disabled, there has to be a discrepancy of 50% between their level of performance and their intellectual potential.

*Emotional Disabilities.* Students who are emotionally handicapped have behaviors that seriously interfere with learning. They experience difficulty with school rules and completing school assignments. Many have a low frustration tolerance, poor impulse control, and low self-esteem. They often seem distractible or preoccupied. They can be disruptive or withdrawn.

*Speech and Language Disorders.* Students with speech and language disorders have a communication disorder that affects their learning. They may have difficulty in oral or written communication and in the processing and production of language.

*Other Health Impaired.* This category includes students with health problems such as sickle-cell anemia and cerebral palsy. They may fatigue easily and also show evidence of disabilities from other categories. Students with attention deficit disorder (ADD) and attention deficit hyperactivity disorder (ADHD) may be included in this category. To be considered ADD or ADHD, students must meet specific criteria, such as poor impulse control, distractibility, and disorganization over a period of time.

# Administrative Support

For inclusion and literacy learning to be successful, there needs to be administrative support for scheduling, planning, and materials. Planning for inclusion begins in the spring when the annual review meetings for special education students are held and principals are working with teachers to form classes for the following school year.

When we begin inclusion for the first time, we have to rethink the placement of students with special education teachers, limiting these teachers to one grade level whenever possible, and no more than two grade levels. We have to plan balanced classes, considering all general and special education students. That does not necessarily mean that the same number of special education students will be placed in each general education class. We need to cluster special education students in such a way that the times required on the IEPs for services can be met, yet classes on those grade levels are balanced.

For example, if I had two students who needed 2 hours of support daily, and one who needed 90 minutes, I might place them in the same class. I would then cluster the students who needed only one hour or less of support each day in another class at that grade level. When I worked with only one grade level of students, often the students were distributed in several, but not necessarily all, classrooms at that level.

Another aspect that must be addressed by administrators is the planning time necessary in order for general and special education teachers to collaborate. Initially, I found some teachers reluctant to collaborate because of the extra planning involved and the time it took away from their one preparation period daily. I found myself trying to have abbreviated planning sessions while waiting in line for the phone or in the cafeteria. However, when administrators realized that for inclusion to work there had to be additional planning time, teachers were given a choice of released time each month or a small stipend to plan on our own time. It was not the extra released time or money that changed attitudes about planning for inclusion; it was the recognition by administrators that inclusion only works with extra planning.

# Conclusion

Learning requires effort and courage. Having teachers and peers respect their ideas, in the same forum and formats as all children, makes the effort worthwhile for students with disabilities. The lines between general education and special education are blurring, and we have much to learn from each other.

## SUGGESTED READING

*Exceptional Children*. The Council for Exceptional Children publishes six issues a year of this journal, covering research findings and current issues in special education.

*Journal of Learning Disabilities*. This journal, published quarterly by Sage, presents the latest research, case studies, opinion papers, and intervention strategies in the area of learning disabilities.

Keefe, C.H. (1996). *Label-free learning: Supporting learners with disabilities*. York, ME: Stenhouse. Keefe discards the deficit labels of children with special needs and writes about meeting their needs in learner-centered literacy environments. The book relates theory, research, and classroom practice to provide a fresh look at the way we meet the reading and writing needs of students with disabilities.

Northern Nevada Writing Project Teacher-Researcher Group. (1996). *Team teaching*. York, ME: Stenhouse.

>   This resource is valuable for all teachers who are about to team or already are teaming with colleagues to meet the needs of their students. It covers issues of educational philosophies, classroom environment, communication, division of responsibilities, and more. There is support for teaming that is working well and suggestions on how to solve problems when it is not working.

Parker, D. (1997). *Jamie: A literacy story*. York, ME: Stenhouse.

>   This is the story of Jamie, a child with disabilities, and how inclusion and literacy enriched her life over a 3-year period.

# Poetry and Prose Read-Alouds: Learning Through Listening

> The single most important activity for building the knowledge required for eventual success in reading is reading aloud to children. The benefits are greatest when the child is an active participant, engaging in discussions about stories. It is a practice that should continue throughout the grades. (Anderson, Hiebert, Scott, & Wilkinson, 1985, pp. 23, 51)

One of my favorite times in the school day is when the children and I gather together with a good book. For many years, my purpose for reading aloud to students was simply for the enjoyment of it. Now I am more purposeful. Reading aloud to students is a sure way for me to become a part of the classroom community. At the same time, it enables me to influence the reading, writing, listening, and speaking abilities of all learners.

## Why Read Aloud?

We read aloud for pleasure, knowledge, and skills. Children never outgrow the wonder of being read to. Reading aloud is beneficial to all children, but it is especially important in inclusive classrooms. This is a no-risk time for struggling readers and writers; they learn simply by listening to good writing and by associating reading with pleasure. Because the listening levels of students are generally more sophisticated than their reading levels, this is an effective way to increase background knowledge and understandings beyond students' independent reading abilities. Good listening habits help students bridge the gap between ability and performance.

The discussions and conversations children have around their connections to the books being read expand their view of the world. At the same time, by connecting the events in the read-aloud to their own lives, students learn that the ordinary events in their lives are important and that we all have stories to tell. The discussions and conversations that center around a read-aloud provide a time for all students to listen to peers, clarify ideas, and express themselves orally. In particular, when special education and general education students listen to read-alouds in inclusive classrooms, they begin to

- develop a lifelong love of books and reading
- recognize what good readers do
- relate the content to personal experience
- stimulate their imagination
- develop listening skills and stretch their attention span
- gain new information
- identify with characters and their experiences
- develop a sense of story and story line
- develop skills of predicting, confirming, and checking
- improve comprehension skills through discussion and questioning
- understand beyond their present reading ability
- compare different versions of the same story
- experience a variety of genres: realistic fiction, historical fiction, fantasy, folklore, poetry, biography, memoir, nonfiction
- learn about the table of contents, index, and glossary
- become familiar with several books by the same author or illustrator
- hear rich vocabulary and expand their own oral language
- explore new directions in their independent reading
- reread favorite books
- find ideas for their own writing

Jim Trelease asks, "Is there a textbook or workbook that will accomplish all this in a fifteen-minute period?" (Keefe, 1996, p. 36). He adds, "Every time we read aloud to a child or class, we're giving a commercial for the pleasure of reading."

If you are beginning to implement a balanced approach to reading and writing instruction, start by reading aloud to students daily. If you are beginning to include special education students in regular class activities, start with read-alouds. Read the story, chapter, or article in its entirety for students to enjoy, and when you finish, allow time for conversation. The conversations among students about what is read bring more pleasure to the experience and give students time to listen to and appreciate the perspectives of others.

Literacy thrives in environments rich in conversation. The ongoing conversations students have with their peers and teachers help them acquire and practice ideas that can be written. The speaking aspect is essential. Much of our knowledge is developed in social interaction with more knowledgeable others, and that acquisition of knowledge is mediated by language. The inner dialogue that guides independent performance begins in dialogues with others and the modeling of teachers and peers (Isaacson, 1992).

Storytelling is the outgrowth of conversation. While listening to and telling stories, all students, but especially students with disabilities, develop language skills, gain confidence, and learn how to think inventively. When they create stories about their experiences, they develop their interpretation of that experience.

When children are read to, they learn about story structures. When they tell stories, they learn to manipulate and control these structures. Comprehension and listening skills improve. The classroom, as a storytelling community, becomes a safe environment in which to take risks, elaborate, invent, explore, and grow (Trousdale, 1990).

# What to Read Aloud

The choices for read-alouds are endless. Read to enjoy poetry and build personal anthologies. Learn about the world through picture books. Read short stories and novels and engage in accountable talk. Read across the curriculum. Read fiction and nonfiction. As this chapter demonstrates, *all* students in the classroom will benefit from read-alouds, particularly those with special needs.

## *Poetry and Songs*

When poems are read aloud, they take on a new and richer meaning. Students who are self-conscious about their reading abilities find courage in the familiar patterns and repetition of poetry and songs.

Ginnie, a general education teacher, often starts the school day by reading poetry or singing songs, sometimes accompanied by her ukulele. She copies a poem or song on a chart and reads or sings it to her class. Students then read along, helped by the rhythm, rhyme, or predictable language. She calls this time "warm-ups" and finds that no matter what grade level she is teaching, this is a successful way to start the day. Over the year, students read and reread their favorites, adding verses or stanzas of their own.

When I had special education children placed in Ginnie's class for inclusion, I found that students who were perpetually late began to arrive to school on time, and students who rarely laughed started to smile and join in the fun. Some of their favorite songs included "Mr. Touchdown," "B-A Bay," and "Down By the Bay."

Songs are especially valuable in convincing struggling readers that they can read. Students usually learn new songs by singing them over and over again, so when they see the written text, they can read it with fluency, a great morale booster. Chris, a fifth grader with dyslexia, had just about given up on reading until I printed out the lyrics to the songs he was learning in a music class. Then he impressed himself with his ability to read difficult text fluently. Teachers need to capitalize on these classroom occasions that invite natural repetition and rereading.

Read poems aloud to set a mood of observation and to model the telling detail. Read several poems from one book to immerse students in the language and themes of the poet. Read favorite poems over and over. Read poems from Georgia Heard's book *Creatures of Earth, Sea, and Sky* (1997) so students visualize the zig-zags of hummingbirds as they sip nectar in flower after flower, and the dragonfly as it skims the pond's surface, searching for gnats, mosquitoes, and flies. The poems in Heard's book make us look closely at familiar animals and consider the fate of less familiar animals such as the Galapagos tortoise and other endangered species.

Read poems from *Baseball, Snakes, and Summer Squash: Poems About Growing Up* (Graves, 1996). These poems about weeding, fishing, doing dishes, multiplication, and other ordinary events, written in free verse, will spark personal storytelling in your students.

Venture into the play of children by reading the poetry in *Lemonade Sun and Other Summer Poems* (Dotlich, 1998). Students immediately relate to blowing bubbles, jumping rope, walking barefoot, and stopping to watch a ladybug, bumblebee, or firefly. (See the Appendix for a list of more poetry favorites for read-alouds.)

As we read poetry, we begin to build personal anthologies for students to enjoy during independent reading in school and at home. Students choose the poems and song verses they like and sign up to have a copy made for their binder. Students like to have choices, and we find that their anthologies fill rapidly. The personal anthologies heighten students' motivation to read and time on task, and they help students with disabilities gain confidence in their reading skills.

## Picture Books

Picture books are another genre well suited for reading aloud. These books are perfect for inclusive classrooms because they span several grade levels in interest, and the pictures add an important dimension, sometimes far beyond the written text. Read picture books for enjoyment and for their wonderful use of language. Read them to help students learn about sense of place and character development.

*Twilight Comes Twice*, a picture book by Ralph Fletcher (1997), starts,

Twice each day
a crack opens
between night and day.

Twice twilight
slips through that crack.
It stays only a short time
while night and day
stand whispering secrets
before they go
their separate ways.

In the richness of this language, we imagine dusk when the sky fills with stars and dawn when "robins hop through the wet grass shopping for breakfast worms." I read the book to the class slowly so we can enjoy the images page by page. (See the Appendix for a list of picture book favorites for read-alouds.)

After each read-aloud I ask, "What did you think?" and we talk about the book, noting what we like and what we notice about the story, plot, author's style, or language. Then we talk about our own personal connections to the book. All the children can participate in the conversation, regardless of their reading and writing skills.

Often students want to flip through the book to make a comment. Danny smiles as he finds the part he likes that says, "We stop to savor fireflies swimming through the air, writing bright messages in secret code." Other children talk about their own experiences fishing in the early morning, awakening to the noise of crows, having to come in when it gets dark outside, and being afraid of the dark. Some ideas relate directly to details in the story while others are connected only by the broader theme of dusk and dawn. One comment triggers another. Katie tells about her stepfather making pancakes every Sunday morning. While the rest of us savor the thought of pancakes and syrup, Anthony counters with, "My morning smell is hamster."

In our conversation about *Twilight Comes Twice*, students talk about a range of topics. Our conversations are rich and filled with the small details of our daily lives. In the beginning of the year, I often start the conversation with some personal connections of my own. Students warm up to this talk quickly, and after a few read-alouds, it becomes less necessary for me to begin the "storytelling," although students like to hear my stories as much as I enjoy theirs. The connections I model are the ordinary details of day-to-day life, such as watching an egret in the bay at sunset, baking chocolate chip cookies and taking them out of the oven early so they are still soft, or enjoying my daughter's cockatiel. These stories validate everyday events and help students with disabilities recognize that they have much in common with their peers.

Often children with disabilities need extra time to talk about their ideas. They may volunteer less so they have fewer opportunities to practice ideas orally. They may have difficulty with new vocabulary, and word retrieval may be a problem. They may need "wait time" of a few extra seconds to form their ideas. The conversations during read-alouds are essential in building their confidence as learners. The vocabularies of students with disabilities expand when they are in general education classrooms.

Picture books, with their short amount of text and powerful language, are a good source for helping children make connections to the text. The conversations around a picture book, whether comparing one text to another or relating an idea to students' lives, are an important part of literacy.

## Short Stories

One of the reasons we read aloud is to interest readers in new genres. Short stories are appealing to all readers but are especially appealing to struggling readers. As Segel (1986) notes,

> The pleasure of a complete story can be experienced in a few minutes of reading time. The shortness of short stories gives them a special kind of impact. Because a short story must be told completely in a few hundred words, the best short story writers work hard to make every word count. The best short stories highlight one brief experience that stands out from the sometimes boring wake-up, eat-breakfast, go-to-school routine of daily life. (vii)

Because there is less text to be read, short stories allow students more time to reread for fluency and understanding, and to linger over the content. Struggling readers may choose to read only a few stories based on the titles that seem most interesting. Choice is a motivator. (See the Appendix for a list of short stories suitable for read-alouds and independent reading.)

In one inclusive classroom, Matt, the general education teacher, and I chose to begin *Every Living Thing* (Rylant, 1988) as a read-aloud. This is a wonderful collection of short stories, each of which centers on how an animal affects a person's life in a positive way. Matt read the first story and we facilitated a discussion with the whole class. We then asked the students to continue reading the short stories and to write entries in their notebooks when they connected in a personal way. We also asked them to think about what ties together all the stories in this book. During our next discussion, we talked about what common theme the students found.

After reading *Every Living Thing*, the students were eager to write their own short stories. As the inclusion teacher in the classroom, I used my scheduled time during the next week for writing workshop, so we had two teachers in the room to conference with students on their short stories. Some of their stories were biographical and others pure fantasy. Jonathan, a special education student in this class, drafted a story about losing one pet and getting another. In part of the first

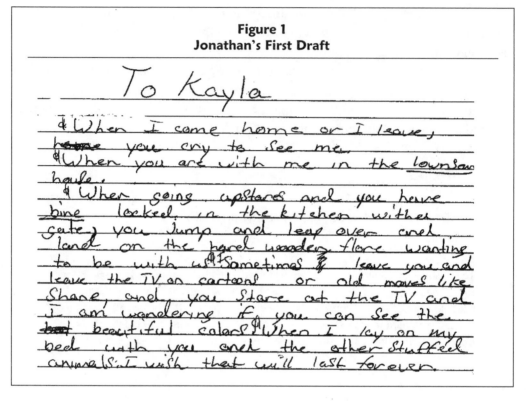

**Figure 1**
**Jonathan's First Draft**

> To Kayla
>
> ❡When I come home or I leave, you cry to see me. ❡When you are with me in the lownsaw haule. ❡When going upstares and you have bine locked in the kitchen with a gate, you jump and leap over and land on the harel wooden flore wanting to be with us. ❡Sometimes I leave you and leave the TV on cartoons or old moves like Shane, and you stare at the TV and I am wandering if you can see the beautiful colors. ❡When I lay on my bed with you and the other stuffed animals. I wish that will last forever.

draft, shown in Figure 1, he focused on his new dog, Kayla, but he wanted to write about both dogs.

Although I walked around the room and conferenced with many students during the week, I spent more time with the students with special needs. Drafts were written, expanded on, and revised. When I met with Jonathan about his first draft, I asked questions to help him think of the telling details that would make his story unique: "You say you really loved Dudley—what were some of the things he did that made you love him so?" I told him some funny stories about Junior, the cockatiel in our house, and he told me some funny stories about Dudley. I asked him to tell me more about Kayla. Later, we looked at his next draft and color-coded his information about the two dogs so he could write all about one and then think about the other. Jonathan also worked with his peers as students conferenced together to improve their pieces. He and I then worked on his paragraphs, and he used the computer for his final copy to help him with spelling. Jonathan's final copy appears in Figure 2.

Matt and I also wanted the children to provide positive feedback in writing to each other as they shared their short stories. We had attended writing workshops for teacher training, such as those hosted by the Columbia Writing Project and those with Ralph Fletcher, and we were familiar with the process of writing

Figure 2
Jonathan's Final Copy

# A Second Chance

It has been a year and a half since my dog, Dudley, died. A car hit him. My love for him was great, and it ended on October 26th, 1996. I cried and I cried for days. He was a Welsh Terrier and we had him for five years. When he died we loot at the different breeds of dogs that we would replace him with but we did not want any dog that we had seen. The only dog that would make my family and I happy was to have the same breed, the Welsh Terrier. We would give all the love to the new dog like we would to Dudley.

The best time that I had with him, that I will always remember, is when I had a metal truck that I would sit in and give Dudley a long rag to hold on to with his mouth. He would pull me around a table. Faster and faster he went, and as he went it became more and more fun!

There were times that I would think about what would happen if he died. Sometimes I cried and I always would talk to him to make me feel better. I told him that whatever happened, either to me or to him, I would always love him. I thought nothing would happen.

But something did happen to him. He died on a Wednesday, after I came home from an activity. It was a nightmare. I felt as if my life was over. I wished it happened to me. I would have died for him.

There weren't many places to find a new Welsh Terrier puppy. We had to go to Vermont to get a Welsh Terrier. It was our only chance. It would take a whole day to get there and come back. We did it anyway. After more than half of the day, we were there. I walked into the door. I had seen her for the first time and she was

(continued)

---

**Figure 2 (continued)**
**Jonathan's Final Copy**

---

beautiful! Her eyes sparkled and she had a distinctive white patch down her throat. On the way home in the car, we decided to call our new family member, "Kayla."

We have had Kayla for two years now. She loves little stuffed animals, which we call her "dollies." She is a great companion. Every morning when I have my breakfast, Kayla jumps right up into my chair, and sits behind me. She loves to watch television. When we leave to go somewhere, we leave the television on for her to watch her cartoons.

Cookies are very special to Kayla. She hides them like a squirrel hides his nuts- so that he can have them later. We find Kayla's cookies in our beds and under our pillows.

Kayla has helped my family and I to move on with our lives. We love her.

---

comments on index cards for positive feedback. Figure 3 shows some of the students' notes to Jonathan.

Students always read their classmates' comments with intensity and pride. A year after this activity, I called Jonathan to see if he still had the index cards so that I could quote them in my writing. As I suspected, he had saved them and knew right where they were.

## Novels

Read-alouds can change students' expectations of themselves and the classroom environment. When teachers read aloud novels and engage the class in oral discussions, students have a model of accountable talk that they can follow later in book discussions and literature circles.

The National Center for Education Statistics/U.S. Department of Education found that students from classrooms where there were more book discussions tended to score higher in national reading assessments (Foertsch, 1992). Furthermore, such discussions help all students prepare to write about what they read on their own.

In a New York City school where I am working as a literacy consultant, the principal, Ann Marie Lettieri, began the school year by visiting classrooms to show

## Figure 3
## Students' Notes to Jonathan

To; Jonno
I Think that your story
Was the besI've head
in a very long time.

To Jonathan
I liked the discriptive
langupge youused like when you
said Kayla hides her cookies like
a squirle hides it's nuts

To Jonathan-
To make this is a very touching
story, I liked the part when uyou said you
thought nothing would happen, but something did.
I accice that no dog besides Kayla, could replace
Dudly, It hit mate how much you liked
the dog when you dirve to Vermont.

To Jonothan,
I liked your Idea of a personal
Naritive it made a really great
story. I Know it is hard to write
about someone you loved that
died, your story was so touchin
it brought tears to my eyes. -

teachers how to use novels for read-alouds and accountable talk. She started reading aloud to the fourth- and fifth-grade classes in September. Many of these students were struggling readers, and attention span and appropriate listening behavior were ongoing issues to be dealt with. The first novel was *Wringer* (Spinelli, 1998). Day by day she involved the students in the story, and after each reading, she facilitated conversations. She asked open-ended questions and the students answered, learning not only to tell what they thought but also to explain why they felt that way. They provided evidence from the story to support their opinions. More and more students joined in the discussions.

At the end of the year, I observed a read-aloud in one of these classes. The students had been studying the Declaration of Independence and the U.S. Constitution for the past several weeks, and now the classroom teacher, Jayme, was reading *The Giver* (Lowry, 1994). The inattentive behavior from early in the school year had vanished. All the students were engaged because their independent reading level was not a factor for success in this activity. When the teacher asked the students what they would do in the situation in this book, they thought hard. Although some felt that freedom was more important than anything, others disagreed, saying that they would be willing to give up some freedoms to live in an environment free of some of the problems they face.

*The Giver* is a book that most students with disabilities at these grade levels would not be able to read independently. However, during a read-aloud they can become actively engaged in listening, thinking, and talking about it. Novels that are read aloud help these students grow in their ability to talk deeply about books, to stay on task, and to feel real, personal accomplishments as learners.

## Bolstering Student Confidence Through Read-Alouds

Sometimes students' seeming lack of skills is more a lack of confidence in themselves and their experiences. A status-of-the-class chart (see Figure 4) allows us to bolster their confidence throughout the day. For example, when we have read-alouds, the classroom teacher or I carry the chart on a clipboard. Students receive checkmarks for listening (L), participation in the conversation (P), and writing a notebook entry about a personal connection (E). Students who have difficulty managing the expectations of the school day find success early here. Simply by being still and listening, they get a check.

As Corgill (1999) notes,

> It is possible to overlook the potential of productive listening. Listening is as much a form of participation as talk. A listener may be reflecting, processing, internalizing, questioning, and planning—all in silence. As a teacher, be an ambassador for talk and a coach for engaged silence. (p. 39)

**Figure 4**
**Status-of-the-Class Chart**

✓ Check for Listening, Participation, and Notebook Entry

| | Twilight Comes Twice | | | All the Places to Love | | | If You're Not From the Prairie | | | Big Mama | | | Old Elm Speaks | | |
|---|---|---|---|---|---|---|---|---|---|---|---|---|---|---|---|
| | L | P | E | L | P | E | L | P | E | L | P | E | L | P | E |
| Alex | ✓ | | ✓ | ✓ | | ✓ | ✓ | ✓ | ✓ | | | | | | |
| Guadalupe | ✓ | | Ⓥ | ✓ | | Ⓥ | ✓ | ✓ | Ⓥ | | | | | | |
| Katiana | ✓ | ✓ | ✓ | ✓ | ✓ | ✓ | ✓ | | ✓ | | | | | | |
| Jose | ✓ | | ✓ | ✓ | ✓ | ✓ | ✓ | | ✓ | | | | | | |
| Richard | ✓ | ✓ | Ⓥ | ✓ | ✓ | Ⓥ | ✓ | | ✓ | | | | | | |
| Serena | ✓ | | ✓ | ✓ | ✓ | ✓ | ✓ | | ✓ | | | | | | |

By highlighting the importance of listening, we help all our students gain an essential skill they will need throughout their school years and beyond.

If students participate in the conversation about the read-aloud, or participate by sharing their notebook entry with the class, they get another check. Quickly they feel successful because they are getting credit for their efforts. The classroom teacher and I circle the checkmark for the entry if we have assisted the student in writing it; this reminds us which students will need help first the following day. Once students start writing independently, we can point out their growing sense of responsibility. For many struggling writers, allowing them to draw as well as write their entries helps release their ideas.

Using status-of-the-class charts to bolster self-confidence is just one of many types of support that teachers can offer. The following sections detail the support the teacher and I provided for three students: Robert, Chantel, and Terrence.

## Robert

Robert, a general education student with attention difficulties, often disturbed his peers during read-alouds. In particular, he would act disruptive with Alan, another boy who had attention difficulties. When I called students to the reading area, I would choose my seat based on where these two active boys were sitting. It might have been tempting to tell them I was sitting between them to help them control their behavior (which I was), but instead I engaged them in a conversation, giving a sneak preview of the book I was going to read, and explaining how I thought they would like it. Sometimes behavior changes faster when we omit the orders to sit down, stop talking, sit up, and pay attention—and let students know in lots of ways that we respect them as learners.

I watched Robert one day while he was writing a personal connection to a picture book in his notebook. He took a bandage off his finger and wrapped it around his pencil. Then he tried to write with his finger in the loop of the bandage instead of around the pencil. That did not work, so he erased all the marks he had just made. He questioned whether a fly was inside or outside the window and noticed a number of bees outside. He began to roll the pencil to watch the bandage flap, then tapped it between the desk and the table. This set up a rhythm that reminded him of a melody, and he began to whistle.

Robert had a completely different experience if I went to him immediately after the read-aloud, talked to him, and jotted down a few of his ideas on an adhesive note to get him started confidently. Before I left to work with other students, I promised him that I would check back in a few minutes to see how he was doing.

His classroom teacher was very clever. She placed a desk off by itself somewhat and called it an office, rather than a time-out desk. Robert often went there to help block out the windows, bees, and excess stimulation he was receiving.

## Chantel

Chantel, a third grader with many personal challenges, was able to overcome several behavioral problems with the support of her co-teachers, beginning with success during read-alouds. She was classified as emotionally disturbed and had reading difficulties, even though part of the problem was lack of attention to task and experience with text. In addition, Chantel had difficulty making transitions from one activity to another. At the start of the year, when Chantel did not come immediately to the rug where students gather for a read-aloud, her classroom teacher stopped everything and waited for her to join the others. In this type of confrontation, Chantel easily outlasted the teacher. It was a no-win situation for both of them.

Chantel, the classroom teacher, and I talked about the problem—joining the group on time—and brainstormed solutions until we arrived at a compromise. We decided that 5 minutes before an activity was over, the teacher would tell Chantel that the period was ending soon. This would give her a few more minutes to try to get everything put away, and if she was a minute or two late for the read-aloud, that would be acceptable as well. If she chose to sit at her desk quietly and listen, instead of joining the children on the rug, that was acceptable too. It is important to let children know that all problems can be solved. Chantel responded well to being a part of the problem-solving process.

Chantel soon realized that to feel successful during read-alouds, she had only to listen and talk about her feelings. She especially loved listening to poetry, perhaps because of its rhythm, rhyme, and predictability, and maybe even because poems are shorter than most other text. So I pulled her into the wonders of reading by adding one poem at a time to her poetry anthology.

During read-alouds, Chantel began listening, reading, speaking, and writing. When she was listening, she was learning to be a part of the classroom community and to gather information in ways other than independent and guided reading. While she was rereading a familiar poem, she was gaining control over text and feeling the joy of independence in the task. When she gave her opinions and connections, she was becoming more confident about speaking in front of others and was respected for her acceptable behavior.

Chantel was very content when copying poems she likes. During this process, she was noticing letter sounds and clusters and reinforcing correct spellings. Figure 5 shows the difference in Chantel's spelling when she tried to spell from memory and

---

**Figure 5**
**Chantel's Writing Samples**

---

Chantel's Writing From Memory      Chantel's Copied Poem

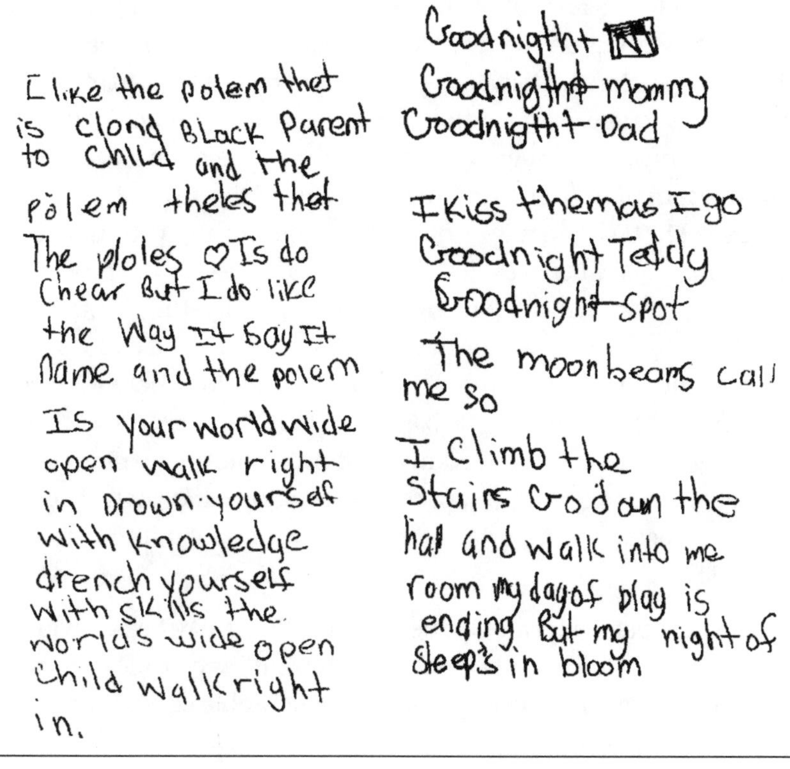

I like the polem that is clond Black Parent to Child and the pòlem theles that

The ploles ♡Is do chear But I do like the Way It say It Name and the poiem

Is your world wide open walk right in Drown yourself with knowledge drench yourself with skills the worlds wide open child walk right in.

Goodnigtht [N]
Goodnigtht mommy
Croodnigtht Dad

I Kiss them as I go
Goodnight Teddy
Goodnight Spot

The moonbeans call me so

I climb the Stairs Go dan the hal and walk into me room my dayof play is ending But my night of sleeps in bloom

when she copied a favorite poem. The poems she copied went in her personal anthology, a binder she would use often during independent reading.

Chantel found her own voice through poetry. With help in deciding where she wanted the line breaks, she wrote her first poem:

**Stormy Evening**

It is rainy,
the clouds are dark.
I sit and watch
the rain fall
and I eat oatmeal
beside the window.
It makes me feel warm.

## Terrence

Terrence also found the road to reading and writing success through read-alouds. For him, letters got scrambled as he read and wrote, which greatly frustrated this naturally inquisitive boy. In the quiet of a classroom, he could be found using the stand-up globe as a boxing bag or leaving the room to roam the halls. Our first success during read-alouds was to keep him in the room, although he sat at the other end of the room with his back to us. We quickly learned, though, that he was listening. Little by little, his curiosity and interest got the best of him and he edged closer and closer until he was sitting with us on the rug. This took weeks, but he was benefiting from the read-alouds long before he joined us physically. The key to bringing oppositional children on board is to engage them through curiosity rather than confrontational rules. Our expectations did not change, yet we gave Terrence the space and time to become confident enough to feel comfortable as part of the group.

Ross Greene (2001) offers suggestions on compromising with noncompliant children like Terrence. He believes that the child is delayed in the process of developing skills that are critical to being flexible and tolerating frustration, and has difficulty applying these skills when they are most needed. The child is not choosing to be noncompliant anymore than a child would choose to have a reading disability. Greene suggests thinking of baskets to help parents and teachers create user-friendly environments when working with inflexible and explosive children. The baskets help in setting priorities for our expectations and goals. The overriding question is "Is this behavior important or undesirable enough for me to induce (and endure) a meltdown?"

*Basket A.* These behaviors are not negotiable. These may be behaviors concerning safety and must be behaviors the child is capable of exhibiting. These are behaviors that are important or undesirable enough to induce or endure a meltdown.

*Basket B.* These are behaviors that are high priorities but ones that you are willing to compromise and negotiate. You are not willing to induce a meltdown, so you communicate and compromise.

*Basket C.* These are behaviors that you are going to forget about for now. You are not going to frustrate the child about these goals and behaviors at this time.

Terrence's first writing was a dictated poem. My teaching assistant made copies, and Terrence proceeded through the school, proudly handing out copies to his classroom teacher, the principal, the assistant principal, me, and other familiar faces he saw along the way. In the years since, Terrence, still a struggling learner in reading, has been recognized several times by the school district and in the local community for the poetry he writes.

For students with exceptional behavioral needs, I use a success chart—a form that allows parents to see the successes their child has had during read-alouds and in other activities throughout the day. Parents of children with exceptional behavioral needs often hear from schools only when things go wrong. In most cases, this overshadows any successes their children achieve. To establish a more positive relationship with parents and to give the child a feeling of progress and hope, I tell parents that I would like to communicate daily and emphasize what the child is doing *right*. I write with details, starting with read-alouds.

One of Terrence's midyear success charts (see Figure 6) shows that on Monday, for independent reading, he read poetry from his anthology, and on Tuesday he read *Dakota Dugout* (Turner, 1989). I make sure to mention the names of the read-alouds so parents can see the topics we are discussing. I also tell how the work is being accomplished. On Monday, Terrence read *The Cabin Faced West* (Fritz, 1987) with a partner, and on Tuesday I taped a chapter of the book for him to "read" as homework. This makes it clear to the parent that *The Cabin Faced West* is a book he cannot read without support.

When work is not done, I leave the box on the chart empty. If I could fill out every box with work successfully completed, the child would not need this behavior modification. I am not trying to report on every minute of the day, but rather to show parents and children that in every day there are successes. I also explain to parents that it is important for students to learn how to solve problems. Therefore, if there is a problem during the day and the student and teacher solve it, we will simply write "problem solved." Although it is still necessary for us to call parents about some problems, by that point both parent and child have seen the successes.

Parents sign this chart daily. Because we are so specific in our brief notes, parents can initiate a conversation with their child that goes far beyond, "What did you do in school today?" They have notes to prompt a child who responds, "Nothing." For example, Terrence's parents can ask him about the reading and writing on the westward movement or how he likes *The Cabin Faced West*. They can

**Figure 6**
**Student Success Chart**

Terrince

|  | Monday | Tuesday | Wednesday | Thursday | Friday |
|---|---|---|---|---|---|
| Independent reading | Poetry anthology | Dakota Dugout | Dakota Dugout | | |
| Read-alouds | Daily Life in a Covered Wagon | —→ | —→ | | |
| Shared reading | The Cabin Faced West (partner read) | The Cabin Faced West (tape for home) | | | |
| Writing | Note taking— westward journal (dictated) | Copied dictation | Note taking (independent) | | |
| Math | Multiplication practice | Word problems multiplication | Measurement (cm, m) | | |
| Lunch/recess | Basketball | Basketball | Inside - problem solved | | |
| Specials | Art | Music | Physical Education | | |

practice the multiplication facts together. Not only does this chart affect student behavior, but it has an equal impact on promoting positive parent-school relationships.

# Conclusion

Special education teachers quickly become a part of the classroom community when they use part of their inclusion time to join the general education classroom for read-alouds. As this chapter has shown, read-alouds benefit all children in inclusive classrooms, especially those with special needs. In particular,

• Struggling learners are able to learn through listening. Reading level is not a factor for success in this activity. This is a good time to begin inclusion with students who have not had such opportunities.

- Students with learning and language disabilities are able to broaden their perspectives and understandings. When all students engage in conversations about the read-aloud and make connections, they benefit from the opinions of others.

- Students with disabilities can participate by paying attention and joining in discussions. This improves their self-confidence and allows them to interact successfully with peers.

- Struggling writers are able to produce short entries in the writer's notebooks after the read-aloud. This improves their sense of success and inspires them to keep writing. In addition, because there are two teachers in the classroom, the writers can receive the extra assistance they may need.

The total time spent daily for reading aloud is 15 to 25 minutes. About 5 minutes of that time is reserved for writing notebook entries, which are discussed in Chapter 3. This portion of time is minimal, but the impact on future writing is substantial.

## SUGGESTED READING

Barton, B. (2000). *Telling stories your way: Storytelling and reading aloud in the classroom.* York, ME: Stenhouse.
> Barton offers suggestions of a wide range of books to use as read-alouds, and guides teachers through the process of helping students develop stories for oral storytelling activities.

Galda, L., & Cullinan, B.E. (2002). *Literature and the child* (5th ed.). Belmont, CA: Wadsworth.
> This book is a resource for far more than read-alouds. Books are organized by genre—picture books, poetry, folklore, fantasy, realistic fiction, historical fiction, biography, nonfiction, and books for cultural diversity—so that you can find books appropriate for read-alouds across the curriculum.

Trelease, J. (1995). *The read-aloud handbook* (4th ed.). New York: Penguin.
> Read what the research has to say about reading aloud and independent reading. In addition, there is an annotated list of the best in wordless books, predictable books, picture books, short novels, novels, poetry, and folktales.

# 3

# Connecting Read-Alouds and Writing: From Notebook Entries to Published Pieces

A writer's notebook is a precious possession. After students enjoy a read-aloud and engage in storytelling, they often write a short entry about a personal connection in their writer's notebook. The entries seem very ordinary, just a few sentences and details about events that are far from unusual. But these notebooks hold possibilities—they hold the seeds for all types of writing. Whenever I want to write a vignette or a poem for a family member or friend, I reach for my notebooks and read until inspiration hits. Naomi Shihab Nye says in her poem "Valentine for Ernest Mann"

> that poems hide. In the bottoms of our shoes,
> they are sleeping. They are the shadows
> drifting across our ceilings the moment
> before we wake up. What we have to do
> is live in a way that lets us find them....

We need to help students find the poems and stories in their lives. Students will find inspiration in their writer's notebooks. We must give them sufficient time and opportunity to reflect on their entries so they can write with voice and passion about the important events in their lives.

The notebook entries that students write after a read-aloud can be used in many ways. We might ask students to reread their entries, looking for a particularly descriptive use of language. They might search for an interesting idea to develop into a paragraph or two. An entry might be the seed that becomes a memoir or the interest that sparks a nonfiction investigation. When students have time to write on their own, they can look back over the entries to find one that they are interested in expanding.

# Writing With Description

When I worked as an inclusion teacher in Elisa's fourth-grade classroom, I spent part of my time reading aloud to the children. To immerse students in what good writers do, I read several picture books, one of which was *All the Places to Love* (MacLachlan, 1994). After the read-aloud, students pointed out which passages they liked, such as,

> Once papa and I lay down in the field, holding hands, and the birds surrounded us: Raucous black grackles, redwings, crows in the dirt that swaggered like pirates. When we left, Papa put a handful of dirt in his pocket. I did too.

After several days of read-alouds and notebook entries, Elisa and I asked the children to look through their notebook entries to find examples of their own good writing. They had been listening daily to fine language in read-alouds, and they were starting to notice the telling details and action words that make writing come alive. Here are some of the entries our students chose to read aloud to their classmates:

> My dog, Molly, rubs against the smooth, comfy bed like a cat. (Michael)

> I am in my dad's car. I'm in the backseat by the window. "It's getting a little stuffy in here," I say to my mom. "Open the window," Mom says, so I did. I felt the nice cold breeze against my face while my twin brother's head leans against my back. (Allyson)

> I am at a tournament party and hundreds of silent gnats swarm around a couple of tables. We are nervous to eat food but I don't care. I am starving. (Joseph)

> I can feel the bumps on the basketball as I dribble. (Katie)

The first three writers received special education services because of reading-writing needs. However, even though it was early in the year, they and all the students in the class were already celebrating their ability to use language effectively.

The children listened attentively as they shared their entries. Although Joseph had many misspellings in his notebook entry about a tournament party (see Figure 7), his fellow students heard and commented only on his rich use of words and the scene he described. Already his classmates respected him as a writer.

Elisa and I each worked with all the students to edit their entries, so that neither group of children felt singled out. In inclusive settings, it is essential for students with disabilities to realize that editing is a process that *all* students must engage in to improve their writing. Special education students who have experienced only pull-out or self-contained programs in the past may have the inaccurate perception that editing is tedious work that only children with learning problems have to do. In an inclusive setting, all students see both the special education and general education teachers as resources, and the special education

---

**Figure 7**
**Joseph's Notebook Entry**

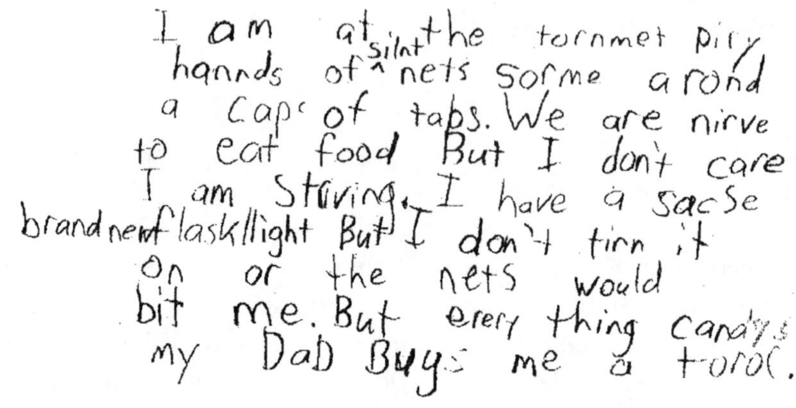

---

I am at silnt the tornmet piry
hannds of nets sorme arond
a cap of tabs. We are nirve
to eat food But I don't care
I am Stiving. I have a sacse
brand newflaskllight But I don't tirn it
On or the nets would
bit me. But erery thing candys
my Dad Buys me a toroc.

---

students become adept at accessing help from both teachers rather than feeling dependent on the special education teacher.

The students typed their edited sentences and we posted them on a "descriptive language" wall. For the next several weeks, these excerpts served as examples for more complex writing that went through the writing process. When students needed to use dialogue, we told them to look at what Allyson did. When they wanted to visualize something, we pointed out Katie's bumps on the basketball and Joseph's swarming gnats.

This language wall should evolve and change as the year progresses. The use of *there, they're,* and *their* in context from students' writing could be added. Errors in grammar that crop up in writing could be addressed. Students are more willing to refer to a peer's use of a word on the language wall than they are to go to a source such as a dictionary. It is a fast and effective way to help students be self-sufficient.

The power of peer support and its effect on motivation is most significant. After only a few months in an inclusive classroom, Joseph's drafts looked quite different. He was using more strategies when he wrote, not because he was learning them for the first time, but because he now saw that all students used these strategies to become good writers. He referred to word lists and back to his reading when he composed drafts. Figure 8 shows the draft of a poem he wrote for his science project. Note how much more closely he was approximating what he wanted to say than in his initial notebook entry about the tournament party.

---

**Figure 8**
**Joseph's Science Project Poem**

---

The Seashore With out Seabirds
If There was a seashore,
With out seabirds.

We Would not see the ponty beak.
Of the Sandpiper.

Or the red aroad the eyy of th
of the black-backed gull.

It would be a deserts.
Were there are no seabirds.

We would nosee a mom gull.
Steels a chick from a nest.

The mom gull would not eat.
This chick.
She Steels and. wreat
We would not see it to,

---

# Following Writing Conventions

As we work toward enabling all students to meet literacy standards, we must give students frequent opportunities to write and self-edit short paragraphs. In the inclusive classrooms where I work, we ask students to develop at least one notebook entry into a paragraph (and eventually a page) each week.

This assignment is an excellent way to help children with spelling and other writing conventions. In my experience I have found that prescribed lists of words do not meet the needs of all students. Although some children do well on spelling tests, they often proceed to spell those same words incorrectly in their other work. Furthermore, although they may concentrate on memorizing words such as *oceanography* for a spelling test connected with content study, this is actually a word they will need to spell only occasionally. At the same time, they may be misspelling *thought*, a word they may write almost daily.

I combine students' need to practice writing paragraphs and the need to be more diligent about using the conventions of writing into what I call "spelling tests." This activity has had the biggest effect on students' day-to-day spelling. They expand an entry from their writer's notebook and independently edit their paragraphs to the best of their ability. I check the paragraph for all the conventions of written language—everything counts. Did they indent? Were the proper capital and lowercase letters used? Did they punctuate? How many words were spelled correctly? Figure 9 shows a spelling test on which the student indented, punctuated, capitalized, and spelled at 92% accuracy.

This is a beneficial activity for all students in an inclusive classroom. Students are writing about what interests them, using words they most frequently need to spell when they write, and getting better grades in the process. Struggling writers who were failing spelling tests on words in isolation are now getting acceptable percentages in their paragraphs. That alone is encouraging. Writers who usually score 100% on words tested in isolation now have to think in terms of whole paragraphs, so they too become better writers.

---

**Figure 9**
**Marked Spelling Test**

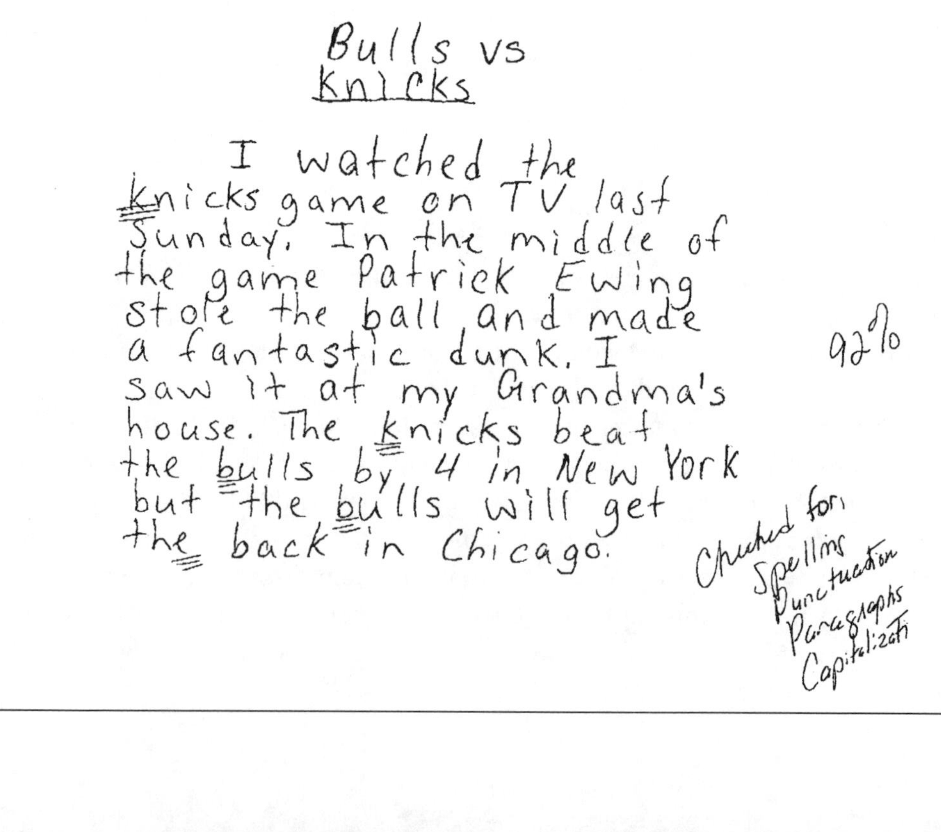

---

Bulls vs
Knicks

I watched the
knicks game on TV last
Sunday. In the middle of
the game Patrick Ewing
stole the ball and made
a fantastic dunk. I            92%
saw it at my Grandma's
house. The knicks beat
the bulls by 4 in New York
but the bulls will get
the back in Chicago.

Checked for:
Spelling
Punctuation
Paragraphs
Capitilization

To improve spelling, I also have students develop a list of frequently misspelled words by looking through their writer's notebooks and drafts. Instead of a word wall, the words are listed alphabetically on a sheet that is kept in their writing folder or journals. In addition, the lists are placed in the writing center and on pencil containers around the room. Because these words come from their writing and are readily available, students are expected to always spell them correctly. After copying them several times, most students know the words by memory. Occasionally students revise the list by again looking through their drafts for more commonly misspelled words. (See Figure 10 for an example of a fourth-grade spelling list.)

Students' self-edited writing provides us with important information on their strengths and needs. By noting what students can do and in what areas they need help, we can plan minilessons for the whole group, a small group, or individually, an important part of the writing workshop. Practice in self-editing also helps students meet state and national standards and transfers directly into improved performance on reading and writing tests.

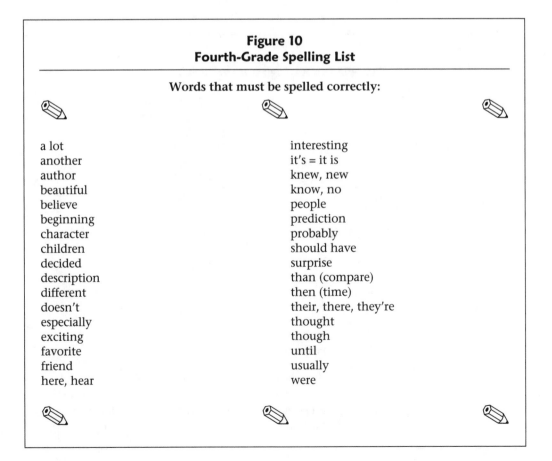

**Figure 10**
**Fourth-Grade Spelling List**

**Words that must be spelled correctly:**

| | |
|---|---|
| a lot | interesting |
| another | it's = it is |
| author | knew, new |
| beautiful | know, no |
| believe | people |
| beginning | prediction |
| character | probably |
| children | should have |
| decided | surprise |
| description | than (compare) |
| different | then (time) |
| doesn't | their, there, they're |
| especially | thought |
| exciting | though |
| favorite | until |
| friend | usually |
| here, hear | were |

# Writing Personal Narratives

Self-edited writing gives teachers important information about students' strengths and needs so we can plan relevant lessons. However, in order for students to become better writers, they need to take their writing through the writing process on a regular basis. It is important for students to have frequent opportunities to draft, revise, edit, and publish their work, so that they can continually improve their writing skills.

If we do not set guidelines for student writing, we may get prolific writers who still are not able to meet the standards set by local districts and states. It is not how much writing is done that makes good writers. Instead, students must be able to incorporate the strategies they have learned in the classroom into their writing. Rubrics provide guidelines for students to follow so they can evaluate and improve their own work. A rubric sets up the criteria of an assignment, the indicators that describe how the criteria are to be met, and the rating scales. The rubrics in Figures 11 and 12 were designed to assess writing. Teachers wrote the first rubric, and the second one was developed with students.

Note that the criteria are listed on the left side of each chart and the possible point values are along the top. In the teacher-created rubric, 1 indicates a beginner

**Figure 11**
**Criteria for Rating Student Writing**

| | 4 | 3 | 2 | 1 |
|---|---|---|---|---|
| Development of Topic | Original, interesting development of topic | Acceptable development of topic | Attempts to develop topic but shows weaknesses | Lacks plan to develop topic |
| Organization and Use of Support Material | Full development of ideas through excellent use of support material | Adequate use of support material to develop ideas | Little use of support material to develop ideas | Does not use support material to develop ideas |
| Sentence Variety | Skillful use of sentence variety | Some sentence variety | Little sentence variety | Lack of sentence variety |
| Language | Uses rich vocabulary and images | Uses general language | Uses incorrect language | Frequently uses incorrect language |
| Conventions | Few or no errors | Errors do not interfere with meaning | Errors interfere with meaning | Errors seriously interfere with meaning |

**Figure 12**
**Rubric Developed With Students**

|  | Professional | Major Leaguer | Minor Leaguer | Little Leaguer |
|---|---|---|---|---|
| Topic | Very interesting, lots of details and supporting evidence | Interesting, good details and evidence | Trying, has some details | Beginning to write but needs to add details |
| Story Sense | Very organized and clear to the reader | Writing makes sense | Most of the writing makes sense but some parts are confusing | Many parts are confusing |
| Sentences and Words | Very interesting words and ideas | Good words and ideas | Some interesting words | Has difficulty writing sentences |
|  | Uses different kinds of sentences | Using some different kinds of sentences | Most sentences are the same |  |
| Writing Mechanics | Few or no errors | Some errors but you can still understand everything | Several errors making the writing hard to understand | Trying but errors make the writing hard to read |

and 4 indicates a proficient writer. I have seen rubrics with happy faces for 4's and frowns for 1's; however, I feel strongly that 1's are inexperienced writers, many of whom are students with disabilities or second language writers, but not bad writers. The students in Renee's class were creative in designing their class rubric, using sports for their rating scale: Little League for 1, proceeding to Minor League, Major League, and Professional.

When students were asked what is most important in their writing, most said spelling. So in developing our rubric, we initially placed spelling and conventions of language at the top of our grid. Then students added that you need interesting details and need to make sense and be organized. After we filled in the grid, we showed students how the order of importance as we write is different, and so we move "Development of Topic" to the top and "Conventions" to the bottom of the grid.

In Linnee's third-grade class, we wanted to model how to improve and expand students' writing pieces through peer editing and the use of rubrics. We read an example of revision from *A Writer's Notebook: Unlocking the Writer Within You* (Fletcher, 1996). The first entry is

Cape Cod is the BEST! I had tons of fun there and I CAN'T WAIT TO GO BACK!!!

After a conference, the revision is,

> Most nights we ate dinner right on the beach. We'd stay up late and I'd fall asleep
> still wearing my bathing suit. In the morning the first thing I felt when I woke up
> was my cat licking the salt off the soles of my feet.

Linnee's students immediately understood from this example how details and
description add to writing. They had chosen an idea from their writer's notebook
and had written about it. Crystaluz volunteered to use her piece for the class
demonstration. She had written a short paragraph about going to Virginia, and I
copied it on chart paper for the class to see.

First we asked students to tell Crystaluz what they liked about her piece. It is
important for writers of all ages to get positive feedback. Then students asked
questions about what they would like to know more about or parts where they were
confused and needed clarification. As we worked, we developed a peer conference
chart, completing the following statements:

- I like the part where…
- I would like to know more about…
- I am a little confused. Could you tell me more about…

As Crystaluz talked with her peers and answered questions, we made a web for the
new information that was being elicited (see Figure 13). She later used the web to
choose what details she wanted to include in her revision.

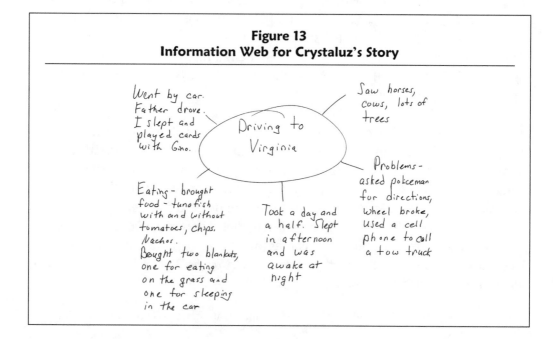

**Figure 13**
**Information Web for Crystaluz's Story**

Next, students practiced having peer conferences and adding details to their pieces. This monitored practice in small groups readied students for eventually having peer conferences in pairs. Figure 14 shows Crystaluz's published story.

When we gathered the students to share their published pieces, they gave Crystaluz positive feedback. First we looked at her draft, and the class thought it would probably be a 2 or even a 1. When students matched her published piece to the criteria on the rubric, they decided she would get a 3 on her writing. Crystaluz, with help from her teachers and peers, edited and revised her draft so that it moved from a 1 or 2 to a 3. She saw herself as a child who could improve with practice—and with the rubric, she had a strong sense of which areas needed more work. As students become used to seeing their work scored on a rubric and realize that they can refer to rubrics to see exactly how to make their piece better, they are empowered to aim higher and improve their writing through guidance and self-initiation.

---

**Figure 14**
**Crystaluz's Published Story**

---

## Driving to Virginia

It was summer when we started our drive to Virginia. My father, my three brothers, my aunt and I all got into the car. My father and my aunt took turns driving. It took one day and one night. I slept in the afternoon and was awake at night. My brother Gino and I sat in the back of the car and played cards. We played I declare war.

When my aunt was driving I saw animals. I saw trees, horses, and cows. First I saw trees. Then I saw more trees. The trees were different because some trees were with leaves and some without leaves.

Then we stopped at the gas station and ate lunch. My dad brought lunch from home and my brothers ate tuna fish. We drank soda. I ate a piece of tuna fish and than I didn't want anymore. I brought two blankets from home. One was for sleeping and the other one was for laying and eating our lunch. It was a long trip and I had fun!!!!!!!!

# Writing Historical Journals

The writing by Crystaluz and her classmates came from personal connections related to read-alouds. Read-alouds can also be an integral part of study in the content areas. Read-alouds make history come alive. Reading aloud to students is an especially good way to introduce students to content for which they have little background knowledge. Students are learning by listening and the pictures and photographs in many read-alouds assist comprehension.

While studying the westward movement in America in Elisa's fourth-grade class, we read picture books, nonfiction photo essays, and poetry to students during our read-aloud time daily. We read about the Erie Canal, daily life in a covered wagon, and the prairie. We read poems about pioneer wagons and the prairie and sang western songs and lullabies. My mother had given me a book of my grandmother's writing during the late 1800s, shortly before she moved to the prairie, and I read aloud the verses that students wrote to one another, such as "If writing in albums/will friendship secure,/with the greatest of pleasure/I'll scribble in yours."

After a few weeks of listening to stories about the westward movement, the students each decided how they were going to make their journey across the country. Would they start at the Erie Canal or at the Mississippi River? What items would they take along? What would happen to them on their journey?

It took a few months for the westward journal project to go from listening and learning to drafting and publishing. We placed the books used for read-alouds on a table for students to refer to as they wrote and drew illustrations. Students considered what a covered wagon would look like, and what kind of toy a child would take along at that time in history. We placed maps around the room to help students plan their journey.

The value of this assignment is that students with a range of abilities and disabilities are all successful. Some journals may have more pages than others, while others may have more details in the writing or more artwork, but all students are learning and meeting the expectations of the assignment. Figure 15 shows a page from the journal completed by Michael, a special education student. (See the Appendix for a list of books and poetry related to the westward movement.)

Other teachers have used read-alouds to teach social studies content. In some third-grade classrooms, students listened to read-alouds about Japan. Teachers did not have an abundance of books about Japan on an independent or guided level for their students, so they read aloud to them. While the teachers read, students took bulleted notes. After they listened and learned, words specific to Japan were placed on a theme word wall so that students could refer to them when writing. Later students used these notes to write as if they were children in Japan.

---

**Figure 15**
**Michael's Westward Movement Journal Entry**

---

4/26/54
We got a wagon and headed for the property.

On the way we broke a wheel going over a bumps. Luckily we had spare. One of our oxen died just with an hour left. Then the children had to push.

---

Crystaluz wrote about a day in a Japanese school (see Figure 16). Latisha wrote about learning to do origami with her grandfather, while Jonathan wrote about a man being old enough to have a wife so his parents took him to a matchmaker.

Children drew borders around their published pieces to represent what they had learned and written about, with pictures of kimonos, chopsticks, green tea, sushi, the Japanese flag, and futons. Because they chose to write on different topics, when they shared their published pieces, the class essentially reviewed most of the information they had learned. Students like choices, and the display of writing showed their creativity and voice much more than if they had all written to a prompt or filled out worksheets.

In the fourth grade, teachers used read-alouds and notetaking to teach about coming to America, the American Revolution, and immigration. Students made journal entries about imagined trips to America, talking about the problems in the journey and in the first few years of a settlement. Because state reading tests have a section for listening and writing, occasionally teachers used that format to help

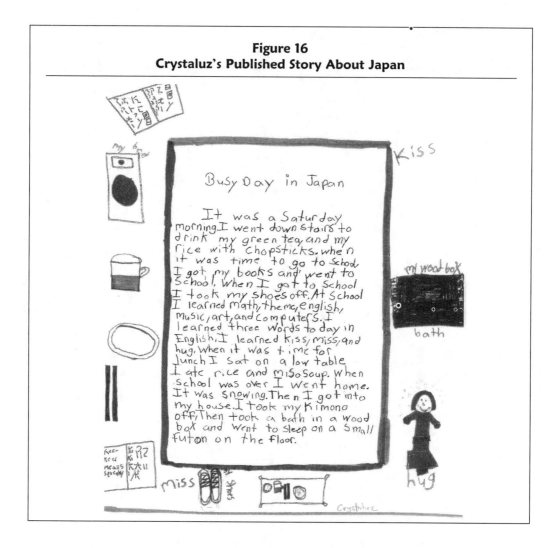

**Figure 16**
**Crystaluz's Published Story About Japan**

Busy Day in Japan

It was a Saturday morning. I went downstairs to drink my green tea and my rice with chopsticks. When it was time to go to school, I got my books and went to school. When I got to school I took my shoes off. At School I learned math, the ma, english, music, art, and computers. I learned three words today in English. I learned kiss, miss, and hug. When it was time for lunch I sat on a low table. I ate rice and miso soup. When school was over I went home. It was snowing. Then I got into my house. I took my Kimono off, then took a bath in a wood box and went to sleep on a small futon on the floor.

students become familiar with the format while still learning about their topic in social studies. In practicing for the test, students listened to a story once and then took notes while they listened to the information a second time. Their writing consisted of filling out graphic organizers and using that information to answer a specific prompt. In this way it was possible to practice for tests while still reading and writing in curriculum areas.

# Writing Memoirs

Ralph Fletcher often starts his week-long writing workshops for teachers by reading from picture books and telling personal stories. While immersed in wonderful language, we listen, take notes, and think of how we might use this material in our classes. In the afternoons, we have time to write our personal stories. Most of us do not think of ourselves as writers. As we hesitantly put pen to paper, Ralph meets with us and sets up small groups of teachers to conference together during the week. Together, we gain confidence in our abilities and look forward to sharing our writing. This is a wonderful model to follow in an inclusive classroom, moving writing from an intimidating solitary pursuit to an enriching community activity.

Iris, a fifth-grade teacher, and I spent part of our inclusion time daily on a study of memoir with our students. Both the study and writing of memoir were filled with lots of modeling and discussion.

We began by reading aloud from Betsy Byars's memoir *The Moon and I* (1996). We had multiple copies available so students could finish the book on their own (with help from a peer if necessary) while continuing to write personal connections in their writer's notebook. This book helps students celebrate ordinary events. They learn how something as simple as getting a candy bar from the freezer is worth writing about.

Memoirs have a powerful influence on students' writing. Isoke Nia (1998), in writing about the power of storytelling and memoir, talks about how writers

> make the leap—from recollection and collection to awe and magic. It is not truly a leap from the safety of our writing notebooks and our memories to the crafting, it is guided ever so carefully by the voices of the authors we've shared. In the heads and hearts of each student should be the sound and feel of memoir and this sound, along with a good sharp pencil, should free students to write memoir. (p. 14)

In our class, we read aloud a number of picture books as models for what people write about in memoirs. (See the Appendix for a listing of read-alouds suitable for a memoir study.) When we were ready to have students start writing memoirs, we gave them a class period to read over their notebook entries from the beginning of the year and to put adhesive notes on a few that might be the seeds of a personal story. Then our writing workshop was filled with students making webs to expand their entry and conferencing with teachers and peers to try ideas (see Stephanie's memoir work page in Figure 17). It was an especially important time to have two teachers in the room. We each carried clipboards with student names and topics, noting which students we had met with, who was having difficulty and would need more conferencing, and what minilessons we should teach.

Students finished their first drafts and shared their writing-in-progress with their classmates. Students read their pieces to their peers, who first gave them positive feedback so they would know what parts were really engaging. Then they asked about specific parts of the story, helping the writer add interesting details to the piece. All students were expected to revise their pieces, focusing on particular parts and adding details or reigning in their story by omitting unnecessary or diverging parts.

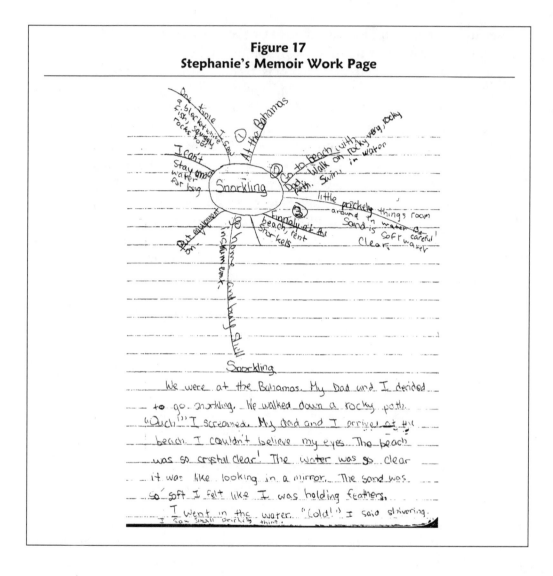

**Figure 17**
**Stephanie's Memoir Work Page**

As the drafts developed, Iris and I noticed that there were some "breakfast-to-bed" stories. Alan, for example, had written four pages and was just beginning to describe the rides at an amusement park, the topic of his memoir. He wanted his memoir to be about the actual experience at the park, so he continued to write, discarding the writing that was no longer needed. Students began to realize that often this writing, even when not used, helps them get to the heart of their story.

We had minilessons throughout the writing process, one of which was on writing good leads. We looked back at the leads in some of the books we had read as models, writing the first lines on a chart. Using these leads as examples, students reached into the second and third paragraphs or pages and found their leads.

Kathryn's first draft began

> Betsy is a black and white cat with a white spot near her mouth. They call these
> kinds of cats tuxedo cats. She is 14 in people years and 98 in cat years. Although she
> is pretty old, she still is very active and curious about almost everything. Betsy is very
> friendly which many cats are not.

After the minilesson, we asked Kathryn to consider the topic of her story so far. Could she turn it into a story about herself? In the flow of the leads she had heard during the read-aloud, she moved ideas and sentences from the middle of her memoir to the beginning. Her revised lead read,

> Sneaky, curious that's what she is. She goes by the name of Betsy, a black and white
> cat with a white spot near her mouth. She belongs to me and these are my
> adventures with her.

The memoir unit was a success for all students, whether they were struggling writers or stronger writers who needed to stretch their imaginations. In particular, all students gained experience in the following areas:

- Brainstorming a topic
- Prewriting, including jotting notes, mapping ideas, and beginning a first draft
- Conferencing with peers and teachers to get feedback about what works well and what needs clarification or expansion
- Revising to make improvements in content and structure of the piece
- Editing for punctuation, spelling, and grammar

Furthermore, all students learned to celebrate the ordinary events in their lives, and that they each have a personal story worth telling.

# Writing Picture Books

As the students enjoyed the magic of the language they heard during read-alouds, they began to incorporate it into their own writing. During the memoir unit, all students, including those who were struggling, found their voices and realized they could tell a good story. Throughout the process they referred to picture books to see how authors write their leads and develop and focus their stories. The illustrations in these books also captured their interest. As Iris and I celebrated our students' writing, we decided to have the class turn their memoirs into picture books.

As a whole class, we revisited the model picture books on our writing table, noticing the illustrations and placement of text on each page. Students noticed that some illustrations covered two pages while other pages might have separate pictures or photographs. They discovered that authors embedded nonfiction information in their stories. Some authors added introductions and author's notes. Some used sidebars, while others labeled the pictures or included maps.

Students then folded construction paper into 8 to 10 sections and did a mockup of their memoir as a picture book. For the next week the room was buzzing with decision making—placing text, drawing, and exchanging art techniques. Everyone was sharing and learning from one another. The only difference among the children was that Iris and I had more conferences with the struggling students throughout the process in order to help them meet the time limits.

Benecia included a fact page about lizards and made sidebars to add historical information about Trinidad in "The Night of the Lizard." Stephanie wrote about snorkeling and added information and diagrams of the equipment that you need, from masks, snorkel, and flippers to sunscreen. Liz drew a map of Wilson State Park, the campground where she found a fort while riding her bike. Tom wrote an author's note about hiking at the end of his piece on three friends' struggle up a New Hampshire mountain. The titles of the children's picture-book memoirs ranged from *The Plane Ride* and *Parasailing* to *My Biking Adventures*, *Teddy Bear*, *Playing in the Snow*, *The Necklace*, and *Family Reunion*. Everyone finished with an exciting personal experience to treasure.

Iris and I were so amazed at the final products that we made colored photocopies so we would always have evidence of the impact of this activity on us and the children. It is now a few years later, but I like to read these stories just as much as any memoirs I might borrow from the library. I also show them to the teachers I am working with and invariably they want to embark on a genre study using read-alouds.

## Conclusion

When general education and special education teachers work together as co-teachers during the literacy block, there is less fragmentation of students and the services are better coordinated with the classroom curriculum. Many of the students in inclusive classrooms have weak writing skills, but with the immersion in read-alouds and conversation, they find a lot to say. Figure 18 depicts the connection between read-alouds and writing. After a read-aloud, children listen, talk about the connections to their lives, and write entries in their notebooks. When they are asked to turn these entries into a piece of writing, no one lacks for ideas. Each student has a notebook full of entries, and there are two teachers in the room to assist anyone needing help. Also, because the students are so interested in their topics, they are willing to revise and expand their writing and to edit carefully, which is the hardest part of all for them. Soon, they *all* feel like readers and writers.

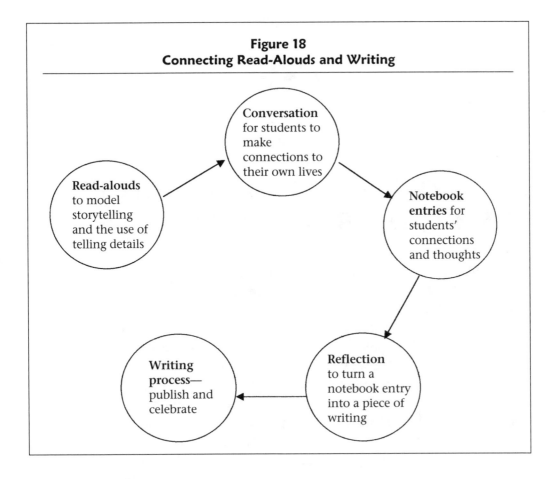

**Figure 18**
**Connecting Read-Alouds and Writing**

**Read-alouds** to model storytelling and the use of telling details

**Conversation** for students to make connections to their own lives

**Notebook entries** for students' connections and thoughts

**Reflection** to turn a notebook entry into a piece of writing

**Writing process—** publish and celebrate

## SUGGESTED READING

Fletcher, R. (1993). *What a writer needs*. Portsmouth, NH: Heinemann.
 This is an excellent book to accompany your writing workshop. There are chapters on voice, character, beginnings, endings, and unforgettable language, as well as an appendix that matches writing needs to books.

Fletcher, R. (1996). *A writer's notebook: Unlocking the writer within you*. New York: Camelot.
 Read this book with your students and the writer within all of you will be released. Fletcher introduces us to the possibilities a writer's notebook can contain—wonderings, memories, lists, dialogue, drawings, photographs, and the writings of others who inspire us.

Fletcher, R. (1996). *Breathing in, breathing out: Keeping a writer's notebook*. Portsmouth, NH: Heinemann.
 This book shows the possibilities a writer's notebook holds. You are guaranteed to want to start or return to a writer's notebook after reading this book.

# Independent Reading: Practicing What Good Readers Do

What kind of books do you remember loving as a child? Nancy Drew, the Hardy Boys, *Anne of Green Gables*? Most of us remember being hooked by a genre or author, often reading book after book in a series. Today, the Harry Potter books are turning children into ardent readers. Recently, as the latest edition hit the bookstores, headlines proclaimed "Harry Potter Magic Halts Bedtime for Youngsters" as stores stayed open and began selling the new book at 12:01 A.M. Amazon.com made a special arrangement for overnight delivery of the first 250,000 books. Times Square in New York City lit up with the Harry Potter frenzy and every news station covered the story. Times change, but clearly reading for pleasure is alive and well.

Children need to read a lot if they are to become better readers. Independent reading—reading for pleasure that is also called SSR (Sustained Silent Reading) and DEAR (Drop Everything and Read)—is a necessary and important component of literacy. There should be blocks of uninterrupted time daily for students to read books and magazines of choice at their comfortable "just-right" level. "Reading practice is a powerful contributor to the development of accurate, fluent, high-comprehension reading" (Allington, 2001, p. 24).

When we consider all that we want to accomplish in our classrooms—helping our students reach the standards for reading, writing, listening, and speaking, and learning more about our world through literature, science, and social studies—we might wonder if it is necessary to schedule independent reading daily. Is this practice as important as planned lessons that cover our curriculum? A look at recent research will confirm the importance of independent reading as an essential routine.

## What the Research Says About Independent Reading

- There is a strong positive relationship between teachers' reports of time allocated to silent reading in their classrooms and reading comprehension proficiency of their students (Elley, 1992).

- Volume of reading is reliably correlated with reading comprehension performance in both disabled and normally achieving readers, even when decoding skills were accounted for in the analyses (Cipielewski & Stanovich, 1992; McBride-Chang, Manis, Seidenberg, Custodio, & Doi, 1993).

- The most effective bridge from low levels of reading ability and higher levels is free voluntary reading, or pleasure reading. Students who read independently at home and at school improve their reading comprehension, vocabulary development, writing style, and spelling and grammatical competence (Krashen, 1996).

- Most of our accuracy and mastery of the conventions of writing comes from reading. Although reading alone will not result in perfect spelling, those who have read a great deal can typically spell nearly all the words they write correctly (Krashen, 1996). Often when we are unsure of the spelling of a word, we write it a few ways and see what looks right, relying on the visual memory developed while reading.

- Independent reading promotes vocabulary acquisition. Readers acquire "small, but reliable" amounts of vocabulary knowledge every time they see a new word in context. The average middle class fifth grader reads about a million words per year, in school and outside of school (Anderson, Wilson, & Fielding, 1988). Even getting only 5% of the meaning of a new word with each exposure, a million words of reading will result in vocabulary growth of several thousand new words (Nagy, Herman, & Anderson, 1985).

- Picking up word meanings by reading is 10 times faster in terms of words learned per minute than direct vocabulary instruction (Nagy et al., 1985). (Rethinking direct vocabulary instruction of words in isolation sounds less drastic to me since I practiced learning vocabulary words with my daughter, Anne, for her Scholastic Assessment Test [SAT]. We purchased vocabulary cards, and thinking this was a great opportunity for me to increase my vocabulary as well, we tried to memorize the definitions together. The next day when we reviewed the words, neither of us could remember as much as we hoped. My son, Nick, a few years older and past the SAT stage, suggested Anne stop the cards and read *The New York Times* daily. He was right—by reading words in context day after day, her vocabulary improved and the improvements lasted. She now has a career in journalism—surrounded by words.)

- The average higher achieving student reads approximately three times as much each week as his or her lower achieving classmates. Lower achieving students read less during the school day than their higher achieving peers, spending more instructional time on other activities. Lower achieving students are more often reported to be reading aloud, usually to their teacher, in a small-group setting. When children read aloud, only one child is reading, whereas during independent reading, each reader reads (Allington, 2001).

- Extensive reading affects reading achievement test scores. Reading more pages in school and for homework each day is associated with higher reading scores. Students who read more pages each day are more likely to achieve the "Proficient" level of performance on the NAEP reading assessment (Donahue, Voelkl, Campbell, & Mazzeo, 1999).

- Title I remedial reading and special education programs often focus on remedial lessons rather than the volume of reading. When these programs do not increase the volume of reading in which children engage, they have limited impact on accelerating the reading development of the children served (Pume, Karweit, Price, Ricciuti, Thompson, & Vaden-Kiernan, 1997).

It is clear from the research that independent reading is a critical component in our reading program. All too often when there are interruptions such as announcements, fire drills, or assemblies, teachers drop the independent reading period for lack of time. Instead, we need to view it as essential to the literacy development of all students, especially students with disabilities, and make our rooms inviting places for pleasure reading.

## Benefits of Independent Reading for Students With Learning Disabilities

Reading for pleasure provides the motivation for more reading and builds the confidence and competence necessary for reading increasingly challenging books. Jason, a special education student who tested in the superior range of intelligence, flourished in the inclusive classroom after he became engaged in reading and writing with his peers. Jason loved poetry, and he used this genre to express the pleasure he found in independent reading:

I was just chilling watching TV.
Godzilla vs Mothra was on
Godzilla was winning when
Pop!
The room was dark.
I hollered "not a power outage.
I want to know who won!"
So I called Lilco
The president of the company said:
"Forget about Godzilla.
It's going to take 5 hours
to get the power back."

"I want to watch TV!", I screamed.
It looks like I will
have to...to...to...hhmmmm?
I decided to take a look
to see what to do,
but then I saw something.
What?
*The Secret of the Indian*
Yes, I can read a book.
And what happened
you ask me
Well: I was up to page 50
when the power went on
and stayed on
but the TV didn't.

The year I had Jason as a student was the first time he had received special education services in an inclusive classroom. He was in special education to receive assistance for difficulties in attention span, organization, graphomotor skills, and spelling. Although before he had been resistant about being pulled out for services, when I explained that I would be going into his classroom for inclusion, he began to cry. It seems he was afraid of feeling even more conspicuous. However, as soon as he saw that I was reading and writing with all students, not just special education students, he began to flourish.

It was in this environment that he changed his view of himself, recognizing his talents and becoming more assertive about compensating for his disabilities. He began to believe in himself as a reader and writer. He liked the poetry of Brod Bagert and wrote him saying,

I know you are a poet and so am I. And well I have a few of my own that I am proud of so I know what it is like to wright one. And I love the way you wright from a child's point of view. So I thought you might like one of mine. P.S. Dream World is non techer edited.

The above poem, "I was just chilling watching TV," was not an assignment, just a poem (also self-edited) he wrote at home for fun. Jason is on his way to becoming a lifelong reader and writer.

Comfortable books include predictable books, series books, and light reading. Predictable books foster reading fluency by encouraging students to use their knowledge of the world and of language (Rhodes & Dudley-Marling, 1996). Series books often have the same characters in varying situations, and this familiarity makes reading comfortable and facilitates comprehension. Light reading such as comics and magazines gives a sense of competence that makes more difficult reading possible.

Light reading makes struggling readers feel fluent. In *Schools That Work: Where All Children Read and Write*, Allington and Cunningham (1996) advocate honoring easy books and choice reading. They point out that teachers do not go for difficult reading. When professional books started having strong personal voices, more teachers read professional books.

Make your classroom library appealing to students by organizing baskets of books by genre, author, reading level, and theme. Include a basket of books that have been read aloud. Choosing a familiar text to reread is an effective approach for helping at-risk children develop reading fluency and build their self-esteem as readers (Pikulski, 1994). Each reading brings more to the story, and repeated readings improve vocabulary, sequencing, and memory (Trelease, 1995).

Rereading favorite poems also helps students become more fluent. Reading along with a tape of a book allows students to access books at an interest level that may be above their comfortable reading level at which they read for pleasure.

## Student Responsibilities

Students need to take responsibility for the material they will enjoy during independent reading time at school and at home. This section highlights how teachers can help students select "just right" books, use their time wisely, and engage in conversations about their reading.

### Self-Monitoring

Students' books should be a comfortable read. We can help students categorize their choices as too easy, just right, and challenging (books they can grow into). Students must have access to just right books in order to benefit from this period of practice.

Finding just right books can be challenging for students. Without our assistance, students may not be using independent reading time well. In the beginning of the school year, I use part of my inclusion time in general education classrooms to get independent reading periods off to a good start. Once students are established in finding the right books, I use most of my inclusion time for other literacy activities.

When I first observed Allyson, a quiet child with language disabilities, she was often off task. She read fairly fluently but had difficulty sustaining attention and showed little interest in books. When I gave her a few Beverly Cleary books on tape to "read," she liked them so much that she started checking out Cleary books from the library to read on her own. She has two brothers and therefore relates to the family stories. Being able to predict Cleary's style helped keep her on task.

Michael was a star athlete but a self-conscious reader with disabilities. When I first observed him during independent reading, he was lying on the floor with his classmates. I watched as every so often he turned the page, seemingly deep in thought. However, when I met with him and asked him to read aloud to me, I quickly saw that he was not able to read the book on his own. He was only pretending to read. We left this book in his independent reading pile (as a challenging book that he could browse and look at for the photographs and captions) and added some nonfiction and Matt Christopher books that were as interesting but were on a more appropriate reading level.

James, a fifth grader with dyslexia who received a lot of support in and out of school, chose a popular Star Wars book for independent reading. Like Michael, he sat quietly and read, looking involved. When he read aloud for me, however, he missed most of the words. I asked, "How do you feel about this book? Is it easy, just right, or challenging?" He replied, "I think it is just right." This indicated to me that he struggles so much in his reading that he is not yet able to assess or admit what a "just right" read is. I suggested he check with the local library to see if they had a tape of this Star Wars book. In the meantime, we found some nonfiction books that he showed interest in. The books had lots of pictures and readable text and were leveled 2 years below his grade level. When he shared with the class what he was reading, many students with stronger reading skills also wanted to read the books for the information they could provide.

If I just watch children as they read, I cannot know how well they are using independent reading time. It is necessary to meet with students to discuss their books. Students must be taught what a just right book is and be helped in finding books they want to read. Students who are trying to read books that are too difficult often engage in more off-task behaviors during independent reading and have more negative attitudes toward reading.

Chapter 5 provides information on conducting reading conferences and completing running records to evaluate whether or not a student's reading choice is appropriate. Over time, students improve in their ability to monitor their own selections.

## Being Prepared

At home, I have a nightstand piled high with reading material—fiction, nonfiction, poetry, and prose. There are novels, magazine articles, and poetry books so I can choose what I am in the mood to read next or what I have the time for at that moment. Students need to have choices too. Their independent reading stack should include articles from newspapers or magazines, their poetry anthologies or poetry books, picture books, and novels. When students have several books to read during daily independent reading time, it eliminates the excuse that they left their book at home.

If we value independent reading time as an important part of balanced literacy, then students must use this time *for reading*. Students should not use this time for looking for a book or browsing from book to book. Worse yet, sometimes students, especially struggling readers, use this time to get a drink, go to the bathroom, see the nurse, or visit the school library for a new book. Unfortunately, by the time they return, these students who need this practice most have missed it.

Help students prepare for independent reading by ensuring that they always have more than one book in their independent choice pile. They can select books during a regular trip to the library or at other times during the day. Establish classroom routines to keep independent reading time free. For example, make sure students get drinks before entering the room after lunch, see the nurse at the end of a period, and take bathroom breaks only at certain times. Chapter 5 also provides more information on setting up a classroom library.

## Engaging in Reading as a Social Process

Although much of my reading for pleasure is done while alone, my life as a reader is social. Whenever I want to read a good book, I ask my friends what they are reading lately. They know my tastes in reading, and usually we leave a conversation with a list of titles. I have conversations with my friends and family about books over a meal, during a commute, on the telephone, and by e-mail. I am returning *Ahab's Wife* (Naslund) to Liz, and gave *We Were the Mulvaney's* (Oates) to Carolyn. Jean and I just talked about *Prodigal Summer* (Kingsolver) via e-mail. I have mailed that book off to Anne while she has given *Me Talk Pretty One Day* (Sedaris) to my son, who will send it on to me when he finishes. My 90-year-old mother called last week to tell me *Tuesdays With Morrie* (Albom) was going to be on television that night. Although we were 800 miles apart, we wept together as this book and movie reopened discussions about her future needs and our relationship. I have bookcases full of books, but I have to admit that I also like the idea that words I love are traveling from house to house and state to state.

I often meet friends for coffee in a bookstore, and invariably we each leave with arms full of new reading. Some evenings we read poetry to one another, sharing our favorites while discovering new ones. The social elements of reading definitely add more pleasure to my reading experience.

As a teacher, there is nothing better than listening to students talk passionately about the books they are reading. We need to give them time to be social about their reading interests too. Although we want students to use the independent reading time to read for pleasure (and practice), we also should allot time for students to browse for books together and to talk casually with others about their reading choices. Conversations help students shape their thoughts, and when they talk about stories, authors, illustrators, and interests, they get new perspectives as well as ideas for books to read.

To promote the social aspects of reading, we can encourage students occasionally to read the same book as a peer so that they can read to each other and talk their way through the book. This process is especially helpful for struggling readers. Latisha and Crystal, 2 fifth graders in an inclusive classroom, received special education services for their learning difficulties. Prior to inclusion, they were pulled out of the regular classroom to read with their special education teacher in a primarily diagnostic approach toward decoding and comprehension at their tested instructional level. They were cooperative about school reading, but their interest ended there and they did not read for pleasure.

Once Latisha and Crystal were placed in an inclusive classroom, their love for reading blossomed. Although they read approximately 2 years below their peers, they read and wrote in the inclusive classroom with the same enthusiasm as their classmates. Because we were using multilevel books to demonstrate reading strategies and content area topics, they felt a part of the reading-writing activities, and this motivated them to pursue reading and writing on their own as part of their play.

One day, the girls announced that they had formed a club after school. Latisha was president and Crystal was vice president. Their purpose was to read together. They took out the same book from the library and decided together how far to read each night. Then they held their own book discussion, sometimes having an oral discussion and sometimes sharing a written response. Their first book was *Muggie Maggie* (Cleary, 1991), and although they were struggling readers, they were joyful ones.

Many teachers require book responses, reports, or projects at the completion of independent reading, so they can be sure students have done the reading. This is one time when I do not have students write about what they are reading. We already do plenty of writing about the books we read during shared and guided activities, which includes reading in content areas, so I leave independent reading free from written responsibility.

Instead, because literacy thrives in environments rich in conversation, celebrate reading by having weekly discussions about independent reading. Students could talk about their reading to the teachers and their peers informally. Some teachers have all the students who finish their books sign up to share on a certain day. By keeping track of the dates on which students share, teachers can make sure all students are completing reading on their own and participating in the discussions.

To impart some of the joy we find as readers to our children, Calkins (2001) suggests sponsoring very brief discussions to nourish conversation and sociability about books:

- Today, get with two or three classmates to talk about your very favorite books in the whole world.

- Today, talk with someone you usually don't talk with about a book that changed your life.
- Today, you and a friend decide on a book you both know that might make a great movie. If you have time, talk about how you'd cast the characters.
- Talk to someone you don't know too well and tell that person some things you notice about yourself as a reader.
- Find a person who's reading the same kind of books you read and talk about the author's style in the book you're reading today.
- Talk with a classmate about when you tend to read and where and why.
- Recommend a book to a friend, or ask for a recommendation.

In one classroom, many students were not using their school independent reading time well or reading at home. With the students, the teacher and I established some guidelines and asked students who would be finished with their books by Friday to sign up for a discussion. To meet on Friday, students decided they must

- finish the book,
- use adhesive notes to mark passages or points they want to talk about,
- participate and talk about their book, and
- respect others by being good listeners.

I planned to surprise the first group of students having a book discussion by bringing a light snack to nibble on after we listened to one another. However, management problems were a factor that first day, and the snacks stayed in my briefcase so I would not inadvertently reward inappropriate behavior. Students not in the group were noisy, and students in the group were disrespectful to one another. As a result, we restructured their sharing. The next week a smaller group of students came to our Friday discussion, and it worked well enough for us to have snacks. Amazingly, by the next week more students were finishing books. Was it the food or the sharing? Probably a bit of both. Management problems lessened as the weekly discussions became routine. Calkins suggests that teachers and students organize lunch table discussions to celebrate their reading.

Some teachers have their whole class share each week, and students share not only books they have finished but books in progress. Students might give an overview of the book, tell about what they like most about the author's style, or even choose an excerpt to read. Reading a favorite passage is a powerful commercial for a book. The best way for students to get ideas about what to read next is to listen to their peers talk about what they are reading. Students begin to see who has their same reading interests. Like read-alouds, this is a time when children are exposed to a variety of books and can branch off in new directions in their reading choices.

For teachers who still prefer to have their students respond to books in writing, there are some alternate forms of written communication (instead of responses, reports, and projects) that work well after students finish a book during independent reading. For example, students might

- leave opinions for potential readers on an adhesive note fastened to the book;
- fill out favorite author or illustrator cards to be arranged by genre in a file box for their peers to review when searching for a new book;
- write in a class journal, copying a favorite passage with the book title and author; or
- write a postcard to a classmate about the book.

# Conclusion

Independent reading is central to a balanced reading program and is critical in the development of reading achievement and lifelong readers. When students with special needs are included in general education classrooms, we must be sure that all students have access to books they want to read and càn read independently. Make this time of day pleasurable and productive.

## SUGGESTED READING

Allington, R.L. (2001). *What really matters for struggling readers: Designing research-based programs*. New York: Longman.
  This book is full of thought-provoking research and suggestions for planning a reading program to meet the needs of all students.

Calkins, L. (2001). *The art of teaching reading*. New York: Longman.
  Pick up this book for a multitude of reasons and you will be inspired. In particular, Chapter 4 discusses the independent reading workshop, and Chapter 17 also addresses issues concerned with independent reading: reading a lot of books with stamina, reading with fluency, reading with friends, and reading in a way that allows us to retell and celebrate reading.

# 5

# The Teacher's Role in Independent Reading: Modeling, Assessing, and Matching Students With Books

Years ago, when we first started including time for independent reading in our daily planning, the professional literature recommended that the teacher read during this period too, to model a love of reading. I thought this was wonderful. As a working mother, I had little time for choice reading when I got home from work. My independent reading all too often was limited to some drowsy minutes at bedtime. Now educators were recommending that I read in school! These extra minutes a day became a luxury.

However, I have since broadened my views about the teacher's role for independent reading. As Chapter 4 showed, it is not enough to model reading in an inclusive classroom; struggling readers in particular need more individual guidance. Some may pretend to read. Others may become discouraged because they repeatedly want to read books that are too difficult for them. During independent reading time, teachers also should be meeting one-on-one with a few students daily to conference with them about their books, their reading interests, the progress they are making, and future reading. All students will benefit from such individual guidance and encouragement, but it is especially important and should be more frequent for readers with disabilities. What you learn during these reading conferences will help you plan your shared and guided reading activities.

For independent reading time to be most successful, we also must communicate with parents about the importance of encouraging their child to read at home, and develop a system to account for home reading.

Finally, we must supply and display the books and materials in our classroom library in a way that will entice all readers, especially those who are struggling. The elementary years are a critical period in the development of reading skills and in the formation of lifelong habits.

# Individual Conferences

Get to know your students personally as readers by having conferences with each of them. While students are reading, observe them and talk with a few of them daily about their reading in an informal way. Some possible conversation starters and questions include the following (Calkins, 2001; Rhodes & Dudley-Marling, 1988; Routman, 2000):

- How's it going? What have you been reading lately?
- How did you decide to read this?
- Is this book easy, "just right," or hard for you? How do you know?
- What have you been wondering about as you read this?
- What strategies are you finding helpful?
- Last time we talked about.... What's happened for you since?
- How do you like this book? Are there some tricky parts? What do you do when that happens?
- Is there a favorite part you would like to read to me?
- I was just watching you and I noticed you were.... Can you talk to me about that?
- What are you going to do next?
- Wow! Your reading is changing! Do you feel how different it is?
- Are you confused about anything you've read?
- How are you keeping the characters straight?
- How can I help you?
- Is there anybody else in our class who you think would enjoy reading this? Why?

## Running Records

During independent reading is also a good time to take a running record to see if the student is matched to the right book. Marie Clay (1993) developed the running record, a record of a child's oral reading. She considers books read with a 95% to 100% accuracy rate to be easy or just right for independent reading, a rate of 90% to 94% as the child's instructional level, and below 89% a too hard book, where effective processing breaks down. An easy book is one in which the child can read and problem solve using known strategies without losing meaning. All too often, when students are not reading during this important time for practice, it is because they are trying to read too hard books.

Running records provide information on whether a student is choosing appropriate texts for independent reading, what cues the child is using, and what strategies teachers should focus on to help the child build meaning. Do they take risks, do they check, confirm, and self-correct? We want to know if students are using the following cues:

- meaning cues: making sense of what is being read

- structural cues: using their knowledge of language patterns

- visual and phonological cues: using their knowledge of letter-sound relationships and print conventions

At the beginning of the year, I recommend taking a running record with all the students in your class so you can get to know them as readers and plan what strategies they need most to grow as readers. Continue to take running records regularly throughout the year, more often with your special needs readers, because running records are most informative when you look at several running records of a child over a period of time.

If you are fortunate enough to have Reading Recovery teachers in your school, they are a good resource to model how to take and interpret running records. Figure 19 shows how to take a running record. (For more complete information on running records, see *An Observation Survey of Early Literacy Achievement* [Clay, 1993], *Guiding Readers and Writers Grades 3–6: Teaching Comprehension, Genre, and Content Literacy* [Fountas & Pinnell, 2001], *Reading for Life: The Learner as a Reader* [New Zealand Ministry of Education, 1997], and *An Observation Survey: The Video* [Koefoed, 2000].)

In the intermediate grades, students are reading from a wide variety of books, so I usually take a running record with the book they are currently reading. I use a blank piece of paper, and I follow along sentence by sentence as the child reads. Every time the student starts a new line, I start a new line of checkmarks and notations, one for each word read. When the student starts a new paragraph, I do too. I put a line under the last sentence on the page so I know when pages end.

When I was learning how to take running records, I first concentrated on making checkmarks for every correct word, writing in the substitutions, and adding "sc" for self-corrections. These notations alone gave me a lot of information to inform my teaching. Within a short period of time, I was able to add the other notations from the running record. To facilitate figuring the percentages, I usually have the student read about 100 words.

A running record can tell you how well the student uses cues, and what strategies he or she is using to handle errors, or "miscues" (Goodman, 1969). Miscues are key in understanding a child's reading. By analyzing the nature of the miscues when meaning breaks down, we can see what strategies the reader is using

**Figure 19**
**Running Records**

The teacher records everything a student says while reading aloud.

| | | |
|---|---|---|
| Accurate reading | ✓ ✓ ✓<br>The house is... | Mark every correct word with a check. |
| Substitution | look<br>like | The word attempted is written over the word in the text. |
| Omission | –<br>garden | Record an omission with a dash above the word in the text. |
| Insertion | little<br>– | The word inserted is placed above the line and a dash is placed below. |
| Self-correction | play ⎪ sc<br>playing | Write the word said, then "sc" for self-correction. No error is counted. |
| Repetition | pla play ⎪ R2 sc<br>playing | A repetition is not an error and often results in self-correction. |
| Told | – ⎪<br>country ⎪ T | If the student makes no attempt, tell him to try it. If the student is still stuck, tell him the word and write "T." |
| Appeal and told | – ⎪ A ⎪<br>country ⎪ ⎪ T | If the student appeals for help, tell him to try it. If the student cannot continue, tell him the word. |

Running records provide information about the student's use of
• **M** for meaning – Does this make sense? (semantics)
• **S** for structure – Does this sound right? (syntax)
• **V** for visual information – Does this look right? (graphophonics)

and what strategies he or she might need to learn. You will want to check how well the student reads for meaning over longer sections of text. Because the student is reading in his or her own independent reading book, take time to discuss the characters, problems, or theme.

After we finish reading, I show the student the completed running record and explain what my symbols mean. If the book is too difficult, we find another one at a more appropriate level, and I ask the child to read a page or two to check it out. Jessica, a third grader, was reading *King Arthur* (Krensky, 1999) when I pulled up my chair for a conference. After a discussion about what she was doing lately as a reader and her reading interests, I asked her to read to me from her book. I took a running record (see Figure 20); she read with 86% accuracy, using primarily visual cues.

Jessica's substitution of *Goldenbook* was actually fairly close. I told her the correct word because it is repeated several times in the next sentences, but I counted it as only one error. Many of her errors—*dresser* for *dressed, naptressed* for *noticed, should* for *shouted, raced* for *raised,* and *hat* for *halt*—were because she used primarily the beginning consonant sounds. In some cases she created sounds that made no sense, yet she was not stopping to self-correct. As a result, she was not reading this book with enjoyment or comprehension.

I asked Jessica what books have been her favorites, and she said she loved the Henry and Mudge books. She went to the Rylant basket and brought back *Henry and Mudge and the Careful Cousin* (1997), a book in the series that she had not yet read. She read two pages for me and she still had errors, but this time she went back and

**Figure 20**
**Jessica's Running Record for *King Arthur***

"Wow!" said Buster. "I've never seen so many people dressed like that outside of the army."

"Look at their buttons," said Muffy, who noticed those things. "That's real gold!"

"GLENBROOK, GLENBROOK, THAT'S OUR SCHOOL!" shouted the children crisply. "GLENBROOK, GLENBROOK, WE WILL RULE! GO-O-O-O, GLENBROOK!"

Robin Hood's father raised his hand, and the children came to a halt.

"Ah, Ratburn...we meet again!"

Mr. Ratburn looked a little pale, but he still stepped forward to shake hands.

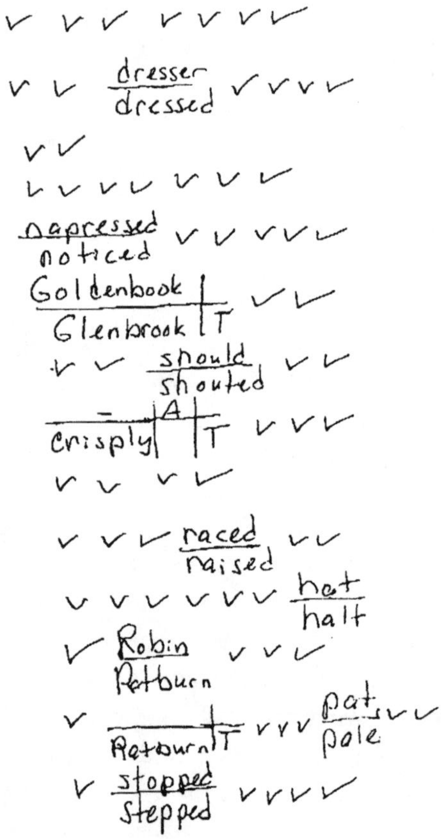

self-corrected in all but one instance and that error made sense (see the running record in Figure 21). When students are reading in appropriate texts that are not too difficult, reading involves anticipating, confirming, and self-correcting. Because Jessica was monitoring the meaning of this text and self-correcting all but one of her errors, she had a 99% accuracy rate.

When Jessica finished reading, I showed her my running records and we talked about how that might help her select books. We looked at what she was doing while reading *King Arthur* and decided it was not a just right read at this time. We looked at *Henry and Mudge* and made a list of some of the things she did well as a reader on her conference form (see Figure 22). She looked at the pictures as she read, she thought about the story, and most important, in this book she self-corrected when her response did not make sense. I asked her what she thought would be a good thing for her to think about as she reads, and she said, "What the story means." We wrote that down and I told her I would stop back tomorrow and

---

### Figure 21
### Jessica's Running Record for *Henry and Mudge and the Careful Cousin*

| Text | Running Record |
|---|---|
| Watching for Annie | ✓ ✓ ✓ |
| One day Henry and his | ✓ ✓ Harry/Henry \|sc ✓ ✓ |
| big dog Mudge were standing on their | ✓ ✓ ✓ ✓ ✓ ✓ ✓ |
| front porch, watching the road. | ✓ ✓ ✓ ✓ ✓ |
| They were watching for Henry's cousin. | ✓ ✓ ✓ ✓ ✓ ✓ |
| "Her name is Annie," Henry told Mudge, | She/Her \|sc ✓ ✓ ✓ ✓ ✓ ✓ |
| "and she's spending the night." | ✓ ✓ spend/spending \|sc ✓ ✓ |
| Mudge scratched an ear. | ✓ scratching/scratched \|sc ✓ ✓ |
| "I've never met her," Henry said. | I/I've \|sc ✓ meet/met \|sc ✓ ✓ ✓ |
| Mudge chewed a foot. | ✓ ✓ ✓ ✓ |
| "I sure hope she's fun," | ✓ ✓ ✓ ✓ ✓ |
| Henry said. | ✓ ✓ |
| Mudge stretched some bones. | ✓ scratched/stretched ✓ ✓ |

---

**Figure 22**
**Conference Form**

---

What I am doing well:

1. _____

_____

2. _____

_____

3. _____

_____

What I will work on next:

_____

_____

---

she could tell me how she was enjoying the Henry and Mudge book and what was happening in the story.

While taking the running record, I did not stop Jessica and help her use self-correcting strategies such as asking her if her response sounds right, makes sense, or looks right. At that point I was gathering information only. However, I usually go back to the text to discuss why the student responded as he or she did and to suggest a strategy.

According to Fountas and Pinnell (2001), the Henry and Mudge books are Level J. I can look in their listing and find other books at this level that will support Jessica's independent efforts, such as the Fox series by Edward Marshall; books by Syd Hoff; the Mister Putter and Tabby and the Poppleton series, also by Rylant; and Little Bear books by Minarik. In many classrooms, a portion of the library is leveled with colored dots to reflect reading levels so students can easily find books to enjoy.

No matter how well you think you know your students, you can always learn something new during an individual conference. Jessica's classroom teacher was not convinced these conferences were necessary—she knew her students well. But she realized, just as I do every time I sit next to a child, that teacher and student both come away from these conferences knowing a little more about each other.

All readers benefit from individual time with a teacher, and this conference feedback is even more important for struggling readers. *Telling* them that they are using good strategies as they read, or that they read well, is not enough. It is difficult to convince children who are used to failure that they are being successful. I am working in some classes where behavior management is problematic during independent reading time, but students invariably find self-control when they realize they could have a reading-writing conference with a follow-up sheet.

I ran out of sheets one day when I was reading with Bernardo. He had read beautifully, I had given him lots of positive feedback, and I was due in another room, so I did not write out what he did well. Instead, I said, "How do you think you read just now?" To my surprise, he answered, "I stink." Because it is difficult for many struggling students (whether they are struggling academically or emotionally) to say good things about themselves, *this paper feedback is essential*. We really want students to be able to monitor their own progress and know their accomplishments, and this written feedback is a good place for them to start. When they learn what we value, they begin to value it too. I have yet to find a student who did not want paper proof of what he or she was doing right.

## Using Conference Assessments to Plan Future Lessons

Use daily assessments taken from conferences held during independent reading to help you plan future reading and writing activities. If two conferences take place each day, teachers should be able to meet with every child at least once a month. These conferences provide teachers with the information they need to support students' independent efforts and to plan shared and guided reading activities.

To organize information immediately after a conference, I use a notebook with a section for each child to record the date of our conference and what I have observed. While the information is fresh in my mind, I fill in a class chart like the one in Figure 23, creating the headings from my observations and noting which students will need what kind of help during guided reading. I fill in these charts with trends I notice during conferences. For example, at another point in the year, I might notice that some students need to summarize or reread to locate important information.

Making notations on these charts only takes a few minutes if it is done directly after the conference with each student. (It takes hours if done at home with a month's running records and conference notes in front of you.) I use the information gathered to plan shared reading lessons, word study, guided reading groups, and homework. If many students show a similar need, I model the strategy for the whole class and guide their application of it. If only a few students show a need, then the strategy can be reinforced and practiced during small-group minilessons and in guided reading and writing groups.

The individual conferences affirm the importance of independent reading to the students. Also, acknowledge independent reading on student report cards. When students see that reading for pleasure counts in the classroom, they believe the time spent on independent reading has importance.

**Figure 23**
**Class Chart for Guided Reading Lessons—Intermediate**

| | Problem solving on words | Self-monitoring for meaning | Making text to self connections | Making text to text connections | Needs to explore a new genre |
|---|---|---|---|---|---|
| Alicia | | | | | ✓ |
| Aree | ✓ | | | | |
| Benecia | ✓ | | | | |
| Briana | ✓ | | | | |
| Crystal | | | | ✓ | |
| Danny | | | | ✓ | |
| David | | | | | ✓ |
| Dominique | | ✓ | | | |
| Eric | | | | ✓ | |
| Eugene | | | ✓ | | |
| Francesco | | ✓ | | | |
| Jessica | ✓ | | | | |
| Kaseema | | ✓ | | | |
| Liz | | | | ✓ | |
| Michael | | ✓ | | | |
| Natasha | | | ✓ | | |
| Roberto | | | ✓ | | |
| Sam | | | | | ✓ |
| William | | | | ✓ | |

# Communicating With Parents

Parental engagement at home—such as helping children with homework, discussing schoolwork, and reading to children—has a strong positive influence on children's academic performance (Au, Carroll, & Scheu, 2001). The U.S. Department of Education found that home factors over which parents have control, such as the variety of reading materials in the home and the amount of television watching permitted, have been shown to account for most of the differences in average student achievement.

In a study of higher and lower achieving fifth-grade students, there was an enormous difference in the amount of reading done out of school (Anderson, Wilson, & Fielding, 1988). Students who reported home environments that fostered reading activity had higher reading achievement (Foertsch, 1992). Reading both in school and at home improves reading performance, which validates assigning independent reading for homework.

Regie Routman strongly advocates that teachers communicate effectively with parents to keep them informed of our practices. To be successful, we must have the support and trust of parents. Reading in the home is especially important. In Routman's *Conversations: Strategies for Teaching, Learning, and Evaluating* (2000), there are many sample letters and newsletters that show how teachers communicate with parents. Some describe the components of balanced literacy while others tell what a just right book is.

As Jim Trelease (1995) discovered, children who had daily periods of Sustained Silent Reading (SSR) scored much higher in reading achievement than those who experienced SSR only once a week. In addition, children who experienced read-alouds, whether at home or at school, had higher scores as well. Teachers need to encourage parents to read to their children and see that children read independently at home. Parents should consider Trelease's Three "B's"—a reading kit involving books, book baskets, and a bed lamp—as a way to encourage children to read for pleasure at home.

## Books

Children should own books of their own. Encourage parents to buy books with their children and talk about them. In many classrooms, students get monthly book orders so they can add to their personal libraries at reasonable prices. However, too many teachers simply hand out the forms without guiding students further. During a recent meeting between teachers and parents of English as a second language (ESL) students, the parents had several questions. They asked, "How do we know what level the books are when we get a book club order form? How do we know our child can read it independently?" Based on these important questions, the teachers met to discuss the best way to support the ordering process. They decided that each time they distributed order forms, they could also give a book review, make suggestions to students, or put adhesive notes on a student's form to indicate to students which books they might like and to show parents which books would be just right. This takes time, but if we want to encourage choice reading, we need to help students and parents choose wisely. I tell parents that if they are in doubt about a book order, perhaps they should go to the library or bookstore where they can better evaluate if the book is a good match to their child's reading ability and interests.

Parents also asked if their children should read only in English or also in their native language. I feel that being bilingual is an asset, and I encourage children and parents to respect both languages. For bilingual families, I point out books that are written in both languages for parents and children to enjoy together. Children's Book Press is a good source for such books.

### Book Baskets

Trelease also recommends that parents place children's books and magazines around their home. Parents can put a book basket on or near the kitchen table and another in the living room. They can keep books near the television and computer, and in the car. It is also important for each child to have a bookcase in his or her bedroom.

### Bed Lamps

Another way for parents to encourage reading at home and make reading a pleasure is to give children a bed lamp and allow them to stay up a few minutes later if they are reading. Many adults end our day with reading, so why not allow our children this privilege too?

## Accounting for Home-School Reading

Students and parents will benefit from developing a system of accounting for home-school reading for pleasure. Many schools encourage students to read 25 or more books a year, and teachers have a variety of systems for keeping track of independent reading. In one system, students record finished books (see Figure 24), while in another they record their daily progress (see Figure 25).

It is interesting to have students help develop these accounting systems, deciding what information would be important to include. My daughter and I both have reader journals where we keep track of the books and authors we read. My daughter's journal has room for her opinions. Because our reading interests are similar, I can read through her journal to find books I want to read or borrow from her. When students share their reading interests, they too can use the opinions of others to find new reading choices.

## Figure 24
## Record Sheet for Finished Books

Name _____

| Author | Title | Genre | Date Finished | Rating:<br>Easy<br>Just right<br>Hard |
|--------|-------|-------|---------------|------------------------------|
| | | | | |
| | | | | |
| | | | | |
| | | | | |
| | | | | |
| | | | | |
| | | | | |
| | | | | |
| | | | | |
| | | | | |
| | | | | |
| | | | | |
| | | | | |
| | | | | |
| | | | | |
| | | | | |
| | | | | |
| | | | | |
| | | | | |
| | | | | |
| | | | | |
| | | | | |
| | | | | |
| | | | | |

**Figure 25**
**Daily Progress Form for Home Reading**

Name _____

|  | Book or magazine and author | Pages read | Parent Signature | Rating: Easy Just right Hard |
|---|---|---|---|---|
| Monday | | | | |
| Tuesday | | | | |
| Wednesday | | | | |
| Thursday | | | | |
| Friday | | | | |
| Saturday | | | | |
| Sunday | | | | |

What did I do this week that good readers do? _____

_____

_____

_____

Circle genres you have read:

| Historical Fiction | Realistic Fiction | Biography | Memoir | Nonfiction | Poetry |
|---|---|---|---|---|---|
| Folk tales | Fables | Humor | Mystery | Fantasy | Science Fiction |

# Building Classroom Libraries

Make your classroom library comfortable and appealing. While reading for pleasure, children like to leave their desks or tables and sit on a rug or beanbag chair, or lean against pillows. Some rooms even have sofas. Your library area should be well organized and cozy. Think about how books in bookstores catch your eye. Some are placed with the cover showing forward for appeal, others are arranged standing on tables. Display books around your room and change the arrangements periodically to highlight new and different choices. Enlist students' ideas and opinions to make the library child-friendly.

Whereas in the past classroom libraries consisted primarily of "grade level" books, we now know that classroom libraries, and especially inclusive classroom libraries, should have many levels of books. We need to have many books at the easy level of reading in all genres, fiction and nonfiction, for this is the level that encourages children to want to read more. In inclusive classrooms, where the range of performance in reading is often wide, this means finding books at easy levels that will interest the ages of children in your class. For students considerably below level, they can practice in easy books, with the purpose of going to another class perhaps once a week and reading to a younger child, becoming an interage reading buddy. As for the children who are reading above level, remember their age. Have books at a level that will interest them and encourage their reading, but resist the temptation to have them choose books that are above their maturity level. A fluency level of reading is not always the level at which the child reads with understanding.

Allington (2001) recommends at least 500 different books in every classroom, divided about evenly between narratives and informational books and also split about equally between books that are on or near grade-level difficulty and books that are below grade level. A fifth-grade class might have some lower achieving students reading at a beginning third-grade level, so it would be the responsibility of the school to ensure that the classroom book and curriculum materials collections are stocked with books at the third-grade level, as well as texts linked to core curriculum standards for fifth-grade students.

When I had a classroom of my own, I had bins of books organized by genre and author. Books organized by genre, such as mysteries, might be written at several levels. Some authors write books that are similar in genre and level, while some write for a wide range of interests and ages.

Teachers have been asked to level their classroom libraries, often placing colored dots on books so that students can readily find a just right book for independent reading. I agree with this, but I feel strongly that at least half the classroom library in the intermediate grades should not be leveled. Readers with disabilities appreciate having some of their favorite books, for example books about endangered animals, integrated with those of more successful readers—and what is to prevent a fluent reader from enjoying a good book that a struggling reader is reading?

In my library, I had separate bins for poetry books, books about sports, and books and articles about animals. I had read-aloud books and student-authored books. In addition, I had a shelf for taped books, which I found that all children liked, not just readers with disabilities. I had an easy sign-out procedure and placed a bookplate in the front of each book, "Return to Mrs. Scala's library," so students would not confuse classroom books with those from the school library.

The bottom shelf of one bookcase was filled with books and old issues of *Ranger Rick*, *World*, and *National Geographic* magazines, reading that my own children had outgrown. This shelf was labeled "Take home and keep." For some of my students, this shelf became the beginning of their personal home library.

For students who struggle with decoding or processing language, there is a certain amount of stress involved in reading. These students are not as likely to use libraries well. However, the students needing reading practice the most were those who were using my classroom library the most. I encouraged choice, so that students could look through a book, decide to read it if they were interested, or put it back if they were not. The idea of choice is always refreshing to students. These newly avid readers enjoyed the smallness of my library where they could look over the selections in minutes.

Some of the types of books that struggling readers (and all readers) enjoy most are wordless books, poetry, series books, and nonfiction, which I will briefly describe here.

## Wordless Books

We usually think of wordless books as books only for emerging readers. Yet there are many wordless books that are appropriate and interesting for hesitant readers, readers with disabilities, and ESL students. Talk is an important part of literacy, and wordless books promote talk and storytelling in a risk-free way. As Cullinan and Galda (1994) explain,

> Because the story line depends entirely on the illustrations, children become much more aware of the details in the pictures. These books provide a story structure—plot, characters, theme—just as conventional books do, and so provide the necessary framework on which to build their stories. (p. 64)

Wordless or nearly wordless books are much like comics. When researchers asked college students about their childhood reading, they found a preponderance of series books and comics. Both were associated with pleasurable reading. The enticing visual cues and simple sentences in comics helped students develop proficiency and led to higher levels of reading and literacy development (Trelease, 1995).

Some of my favorites for students in the intermediate grades are

*The Snowman* (Briggs, 1987)

*A Boy, a Dog, and a Frog* (Mayer, 1992)

*Dreams* (Spier, 1986)

*We the People* (Spier, 1999)

*Ben's Dream* (Van Allsburg, 1982)

*Tuesday* (Wiesner, 1991)

*Sector 7* (Wiesner, 1999)

In one fifth-grade classroom in New York City, the students were learning about the American Revolution and the U.S. Constitution. We had Fritz's *Shh! We're Writing the Constitution* (1998) and some thick texts in the room, but the book that brought this information to life for students was Spier's *We the People* (1991). After the introduction, the book contains illustrations that visually describe each phrase of the Preamble, both then and now, and then includes the documents. Through the wordless pages, students begin to realize what the phrases mean: "in order to form a more perfect union, establish justice, insure the domestic tranquility...." One can spend hours just looking at two pages, comparing what life was like then to now. What is the same? How is it different? Today, I wonder how I ever taught this information before I found this book. Students who have read *We the People* on their own and with others will forever repeat these words with new meaning.

## *Poetry*

When we look for multilevel reading material for inclusive classrooms, there is no better source than poetry books. Students also love to refer to their personal anthologies during independent reading.

Although I have found that all students respond to poetry, it is an especially good source for the readers with disabilities for the following reasons:

- There is no grade level in poetry. Special education students and struggling learners perform equally as well as general education students in this genre.
- Poems are spatially pleasing, often with phrases or just a few words on a line with lots of white space. This gives children with reading difficulties a sense of visual control.
- Poems can be short, powerful, and easy to read.
- Poetry can impart an important message in a few words so it maintains integrity.
- Poetry helps struggling readers become more fluent. Poems are meant to be read and reread, and rereading promotes fluency.
- Poems have predictability—repeated phrases and patterns of rhythm and rhyme. Struggling readers gain confidence in their ability to decode by reading predictable texts.
- A lot of poetry can be discovered in a short period of time.
- When students read poetry, they feel successful and become motivated to increase time spent on reading. Their reading improves, which also translates into improved reading in other genres.
- Readers of poetry become writers of poetry.
- Poetry can be an integral part of reading, writing, social studies, science, and math.

Chantel, the student with emotional disabilities introduced in Chapter 2, often was oppositional. One day when she was looking for a book for independent reading, I showed her the poetry book *Families: Poems Celebrating the African American Experience* (Strickland & Strickland, 1994) and read her a few of my favorites. She immediately signed out the book. The next day she read several poems to me, skipping around the book, which she already knew well, finding one poem after another that she loved. By the third day, she was making a "book cover" and copying many of the poems so she will always have a copy. When I attended a conference that week and saw Michael Strickland, I gave him photocopies of her pages of copying, and he wrote her a personal message. What could be more motivating!

Brianna, the child quoted in Chapter 1 as saying her response "clear as the wind," was reading *Spin a Soft Black Song* (Giovanni, 1987). She liked the poem about "two friends" and we enjoyed it together. Months later, she and Kristen decided to write a poem together, and Brianna found the book. She explained her idea to Kristen and they began to write and giggle. Soon, they shared their rendition of "Two Best Friends":

**Two Best Friends**

Brianna and Kristen have,
two jackets
103 braids
two pairs of sneakers
one necklace
one bracelet
four pierced ears
two good senses of humor
two wide smiles
and the best of friendships.

## Series Books

As teachers and parents, we strive to expose our children to good literature. We become concerned when they show more interest in Sweet Valley High or Goosebumps books than the classics. Why do children like these books so much? According to Trelease (1995),

> There appears to be a need for familiar characters, text, and situations that are predictable enough to be nonthreatening, inviting, and mindless enough to allow a young reader to become proficient and fluent, and to meet lots of words without having to contend with subplots and character development. (p. 201)

Our classrooms are becoming increasingly heterogeneous. Many readers enjoy series books, but these books are especially supportive of readers with disabilities and ESL readers of all ages who benefit from narrowing their reading to one author and genre, because the knowledge gathered in previously read texts makes the reading immediately accessible.

In *Beyond Leveled Books: Supporting Transitional Readers in Grades 2–5* (2001), Syzmusiak and Sibberson devote several pages on the supports in series books, such as text setup, chapter titles, hooks, dialogue, and pictures. They also compare series books with similar features—animal characters with human experiences, human characters with an animal companion, mystery-adventure themes, adventure with friends, humorous stories, and stories that take the reader back in time. Listed under mystery-adventure themes are Adler for his Cam Jansen series, Osborne for the Magic Tree House adventures, Levy for Invisible Ink and also Something Queer Mysteries, Roy for A to Z Mysteries, and Preller for his Jigsaw Jones series. (See the Appendix for a list of popular series books.)

## Nonfiction

There is a definite need and place for more nonfiction in our classroom libraries. I work in schools where a great deal of time and effort has been made to level part of each classroom library so that students can reach quickly for a just right book. For many students, leveling provides them with series books they love to read. However, there are other students, especially older students with reading disabilities, who are no longer interested in the series books on their reading level. For these students, nonfiction books often pique their interest. (Some nonfiction books and magazines of interest to struggling readers [and all readers] are listed in the Appendix.)

One day in a fifth-grade classroom, I was modeling independent reading conferences when I noticed Brandon with his head down on the desk. I asked him why he was not reading, and he told me he did not like books. He had a series book in front of him, but he said he did not like it. When I asked him what he might be interested in, he did not answer. I started suggesting topics, and when I asked if he liked to read about animals, he lifted his head.

Fortunately, at that moment a student next to him said he had just finished one of the *Zoobooks* magazines. He slid it toward Brandon, who started to leaf through it and read. To determine whether the level was a good match for Brandon, we did a running record. He chose to read about the blue whale and knew words such as *continent* and *Australia*. When he finished a passage, he told us that he had been to the Museum of Natural History and had seen the model of the blue whale. I told him the whale display had been my son's favorite room in the museum, and we talked some more. He explained that he had maps at home, and asked his teacher if she would like him to bring them in. Nonfiction had awakened this child during independent reading.

Later, Brandon's teacher and I looked at our running records. The first surprise was how much better he did on this running record than on one taken 2 weeks earlier. She had used a page from a basal series so she could quickly level the results. We knew Brandon had not progressed years in 2 weeks. What we surmised from this discrepancy was that he was not interested in the story he read from the basal and that when he was interested, he put in more effort with telling results.

Some nonfiction books can be read much like fiction books. Many nonfiction picture books tell stories using the same print features as fictional texts. But other nonfiction books have very different features, such as different size and colored fonts, photographs and labeled pictures, time lines, maps, graphs, introductions, prologues, author's notes, and sidebars. We can model strategies for reading nonfiction text during shared and guided reading.

# Conclusion

Too often, teachers provide students with time for independent reading without any direction or guidance. The daily reading conferences I advocate give us valuable information about our students and their needs. This is a time to get personal—to learn about the student, find out about his or her interests and curiosities, and take the time to make good matches between books and students.

Communication with parents also helps make independent reading a success. Parents can help by encouraging students to read at home, discussing books with their children, and serving as role models by reading for pleasure and information.

Finally, teachers in inclusive classrooms need to set up a classroom library that is appealing and easy to use. When all students have a choice of books they can read with success, they develop self-confidence. Independent reading is only a good predictor of reading success if students enjoy what they are reading, making them want to read more.

## SUGGESTED READING

It takes a lot of time to find the right level book or author to interest a student. Several books can help in the search—both in saving time and in broadening our knowledge of reading materials. I suggest that teachers take this list to their administrators and ask that some be added to (or used to start) a professional library for teachers:

Cullinan, B.E. (2000). *Let's read about: Finding books they'll love to read* (2nd ed.). New York: Scholastic.

> Written as a guide for parents, this book is equally valuable for teachers. It is a good book to help make the home-school connection in reading programs.

Graves, M.F., & Graves, B.B. (1994). *Scaffolding reading experiences: Designs for student success.* Norwood, MA: Christopher-Gordon.

> The authors provide suggestions for meeting the reading needs of all learners with a multitude of strategies. Many examples of activities are presented with the goal,

rationale, procedure, adaptation, and reflections. The booklist is by author or title, grade level, and subject.

Hart-Hewins, L., & Wells, J. (1999). *Better books! Better readers! How to choose, use and level books for children in the primary grades*. York, ME: Stenhouse.

This is a practical book with lessons and leveled book suggestions that readers beyond the primary grades will enjoy. Suggestions for classroom organization, centers, and categorizing your classroom book collection abound.

Toussaint, P. (1999). *Great books for African-American children*. New York: Penguin.

In this guide, children's books are divided by age level—very young, 4 to 8, 8 to 11, preteens and young adults—with extensive annotations about each book and good suggestions for all children. The book's theme index is a valuable resource.

# 6

# Shared Reading: Modeling What Good Readers Do

Shared reading, a concept based on research by Don Holdaway (1979), provides children with an enjoyable reading experience, introduces them to a variety of authors and illustrators and the way these communicators craft meaning, and teaches children systematically and explicitly how to be readers and writers themselves. Students are involved in collaborative meaning making as the teacher models effective reading strategies, skills, and behaviors, and invites active participation. The books used are readily available so students have the opportunity to reread familiar books in paired and independent situations as well as in the larger group (Parkes, 2000).

In the shared book experience, all students have access to print, either with Big Books or by using charts or overhead transparencies to enlarge the print. The teacher reads *to* and *with* students while encouraging them to be able to read by themselves with increasing independence. Often the demonstration of reading strategies is connected to writing, which is also modeled.

## Shared Reading in the Intermediate Grades

Modeling and guiding our students in reading and writing is as essential in the intermediate grades as it is for beginning readers and writers. What does shared reading look like in intermediate classrooms? Poems, songs, stories, plays, and informational texts are used to engage children in pleasurable experiences with books in a supportive environment. Teachers are modeling specific strategies such as prediction and visualization, investigating words and forming generalizations during word study, and exploring literary elements such as character, plot, and theme.

Fiction and nonfiction are used to inform and connect literacy to content area study in science, social studies, and math. For example, teachers might demonstrate the scientific method of inquiry in preparation for science research during shared reading. Students respond orally, through illustrations, and in writing.

The shared reading experience, like the other components of balanced literacy, provides teachers with opportunities to "kidwatch" (Goodman, 1978). Look closely at your students—are they enjoying the book, are they using strategies to construct meaning, are they using multiple cueing systems? This informal type of assessment will help you plan across the curriculum.

The materials used for shared reading are chosen with a particular focus, based on the teacher's assessment of students' needs. Three questions will help plan for shared reading:

1. What strategies and skills do my students need to know and use?
2. What material will I use to demonstrate these strategies and skills?
3. Will it engage my students and invite rereadings?

By keeping these questions in mind, we find prose, poetry, fiction, and nonfiction to model the learning strategies students need through meaningful text.

Shared reading is an important time for the general education and special education teacher to collaborate. In the beginning of the school year, teachers might begin collaborating during read-alouds and independent reading so they can quickly get to know all the students. However, most of the time that the special education teacher is collaborating in the inclusive classroom during the year will be for shared and guided reading-writing activities.

Students with disabilities benefit from activities in which teachers and students read and think aloud together in a shared text. In this supportive environment, students can join in the reading as they feel able to do so. They can access information and thought processes in a group that they might not experience independently. Struggling students, with their peers, learn how to make statements and provide supporting details, figure out the author's purpose or theme, predict and confirm or readjust their predictions, and match reading strategies to the type of text being read. They know they are doing the same important work as the rest of the class. For too long, when special education students were pulled out of the classroom for explicit skill instruction in reading and writing that was not connected to their experiences, they felt different and often saw their work as separate and in a less positive light. Spending time learning skills in isolation does not work, because students tend not to connect the skills to real reading or their lives, and they are hurt by being kept away from challenging, high-level reading discussions (Cooper, 1997). Many students lose interest in what is being taught during this type of instruction.

Even though students with disabilities may read several levels below their peers, they benefit from inclusion during shared reading and writing activities. If I use a well-written yet less complex book to demonstrate the strategies and thinking skills I want to develop, all students will be able to access the information. Students can then practice the strategy or skill using books on their independent or guided reading levels. For example, all the students learning about self-questioning during a shared reading lesson will practice the same strategy in guided or independent reading while using different nonfiction books, novels, picture books, or poetry. The strategies students learn during shared reading are the same; the difficulty of the text they use to practice the strategies differs. Teachers can monitor how students are applying their learning in their individual or small-group work by asking them to jot down the questions they ask themselves on adhesive notes and leave them in the text as they read.

When students with disabilities were pulled out of the general education classroom for services, the goal was to parallel the curriculum of the general education class through modification of assignments. It was a deficit model—we assessed the disabilities and provided individualized or small-group remediation. Pulling out students from their regular class was an accepted practice for many years, but special education students were not thriving.

My students' reading and writing achievements improved when I began to use trade books, response journals, and other components of a balanced literacy philosophy. When I was able to provide special education services in general education classrooms, students were even more successful in overcoming and compensating for their reading and writing disabilities. My experiences in inclusive classrooms have taught me the following:

- Constructing meaning in a relaxed setting with peers during shared reading and writing helps improve the self-esteem of special education students. When they see strategies being demonstrated to the whole class, they realize these are important tools for all learners and that all readers use essentially the same strategies to construct meaning from text.

- During shared reading and writing, teachers model learning strategies and students practice what has been modeled in an atmosphere of support and encouragement. Because there is an emphasis on approximations and on what students are doing well, all students expect and receive positive feedback.

- When teachers and students think aloud, students with disabilities learn how to listen and talk to others to clarify what they do not understand or to extend what they already know. They can access a text that otherwise would be too difficult.

- When teachers co-teach during inclusion periods each day, students with special needs and general education students learn to ask for help from both teachers and become less dependent on one source of assistance.

- When teachers collaborate to meet the needs of all children, each teacher is learning from the other—behavior management techniques, organizational structures, and subject area expertise. The classroom becomes a richer environment.

# Helping Students Develop Reading Strategies

We use more than one cueing system when we read. We construct meaning by using our personal knowledge about the world and by noticing visual and phonological cues. We self-monitor for meaning by asking continually if what we are reading makes sense (semantic awareness) and if it sounds right (syntactical-grammatical awareness).

It is important for students to knowingly use strategies and skills. However, it is not enough to tell students the skills and strategies they need to become better readers and writers. Instead, students need to learn in print-rich classrooms where they can look around to find evidence of what good readers and writers and thinkers do. For example, every time you model a specific strategy for shared reading, add it to a chart labeled "What Good Readers Do" (see Figure 26). Make sure the chart is available for future reference so readers can refer to it at any time for a reminder of strategies to try. There is a feeling of accomplishment as students see the list grow.

When I first began consulting in some urban schools where many students were not meeting local and state performance standards, what surprised me most

---

### Figure 26
### What Good Readers Do

- Choose books on an appropriate reading level
- Set a purpose for reading
- Skim pictures, chapter titles, and headings for information
- Use visualization to understand reading
- Use context cues and graphophonemic knowledge to learn new words
- Recall details from what is read
- Predict and confirm/readjust predictions
- Ask questions and read or reread to answer them
- Use prior knowledge to understand what is read
- Make connections to reading
- Form opinions and support them from the text
- Adjust reading rate to type of reading
- Self-monitor, ask for help when needed
- Make inferences
- Draw conclusions
- Compare and contrast
- Want to read more

was that comprehension was the predominant problem, not decoding. Many students read rather fluently but were not reading for meaning. To me, the fluency suggested that these children had read a lot. But had they read material that was interesting and relevant enough to them that they wanted to read for meaning? Had they been taught to use strategies that heighten meaning making?

During shared reading periods, it is important to think aloud together and demonstrate how to be good readers by modeling before-, during-, and after-reading strategies, and allotting students time for practice. In particular, here are three lists of strategies that teachers need to model and help students practice.

**Before-Reading Strategies**
Preview text
Make predictions
Skim through material
Set a purpose for reading
Ask questions
Activate prior knowledge
Make personal connections

**During-Reading Strategies**
Visualize
Verify predictions/adjust predictions/make new ones
Answer questions/ask new ones
Self-monitor for understanding (Does this make sense?)
Self-correct, reread, read ahead
Adjust reading rate to material
Discuss text, take notes
Use punctuation to assist meaning

**After-Reading Strategies**
Reflect on reading
Confirm, adjust predictions
Skim, reread for understanding
Locate specific information
Summarize main points
Retell
Respond to reading—talking, writing, drawing, performing
Feel successful and want to read more

Teachers continually evaluate students during the day to help them plan specific shared and guided reading activities based on student needs. With this information, they plan for whole-class, small-group, or one-on-one instruction.

## *Modeling Prediction*

To demonstrate the many ways we use prediction as a way to think as we read for meaning, I used the Big Book *The Greedy Goat* (Bolton, 1996) with an inclusive third-grade class. Folk tales such as this one are an excellent source for introducing intermediate-grade students to prediction. Galda and Cullinan (2002) and Parkes (2000) point out that folk tales tend to contain the following characteristics:

- The heroes and heroines have virtues such as cleverness and bravery.
- The stories contain very little ambiguity: Good is good, evil is evil.
- Tales help students maintain meaning over longer stretches of continuous text.
- The predictable language supports the development of phrasing and fluency.
- The structure of the tales is clear-cut with a beginning, middle, and end.
- The conflict is identified early.
- The ending resolves the problem without complications.
- Different versions of folk tales can be compared to see how different authors and cultures develop setting, plot, characterization, and illustrations.
- Tales are a good genre to encourage rereading.
- A tale can be used for an authentic test preparation activity when children need to recall sequences of events; identify beginning, middle, and end; or interpret the dialogue of a character.

Before I started to read *The Greedy Goat*, I asked students to look at the cover, which states that this is a traditional tale retold by Faye Bolton. They saw a goat, the title, and the words *traditional tale*. From that information and some prior experience with folk tales, students predicted that this story could be about a goat, maybe the goat had a problem, maybe the goat was the problem, and that the problem would get solved. They were not sure about the meaning of *greedy*, but some thought it might mean *selfish*. They also thought the story might begin "Once upon a time...."

The tale starts, "One day an old woman was cleaning her house." The children confirmed that tales do start like "Once upon a time" and "One day." The old woman in the story makes a creamy rice pudding, places it on the table to cool, and goes outside. Here students predicted what would happen next. Prediction is fun when students—especially struggling students lacking confidence—realize that predicting is not a matter of being right or wrong but of reading on to confirm your prediction or readjust your thinking. Already some students were thinking that the goat is the problem, not the character having the problem.

The goat enters the house and several animals come along to help the woman get rid of it. In each segment, the animals make a sound such as CLOP-CLOP-CLOP or PAD-PAD-PAD, and there is a pattern in the conversations. The last two lines of each sequence end with

> Off with you, I'm a fighting goat.
> My two big horns will rip your ____.

I had covered the last word with an adhesive note. Most children predicted *coat* because they thought it was part of a rhyme and *coat* made sense. One child suggested *throat*, and they agreed that would make sense, too. When I uncovered the first letter and they all decided that the word was *coat*, we checked and confirmed their thinking. I pointed out that they used several cueing systems: the rhyming pattern, making sense, and the beginning letter. We continued with the story, and many began reading with me when they saw the words *Off with you....*

Next I asked them to predict the covered word on another page:

This scared the dog, and it _____off down the road.

Students predicted *ran* and *hurried*, and we uncovered the word to find *scampered*. We talked about how our predictions all made sense, but the author chose another word. We continued predicting the ending word in rhyming couplets and the ways in which animals moved. (Their favorite was *rocketed*.) We predicted whether each animal would be successful in getting the goat out of the house. To make a not-too-long story short, it was the mouse (small and unlikely but clever) that was successful in ousting the goat from the old woman's house.

After the story we discussed the tale and what we had learned about predicting as we read. I gave each student an adhesive note on which to write about a part where he or she used prediction in the story. The classroom teacher and I moved around the room, making sure that everyone completed a few sentences. Students with less confidence drew and wrote a few words, sometimes with help from a classmate. As students read their responses and placed their adhesive notes on a class chart, their teacher placed a check by their names on the status-of-the-class sheet.

We asked students to think about prediction as a strategy over the next few days when they read and to write their predictions on adhesive notes and leave them in their books. If they confirmed or readjusted their prediction, they could move the adhesive note to that spot. In this way, we were able to look at their books and see how well they were using prediction to construct meaning.

The Big Book was placed in our library so students could reread it independently or in pairs. As a class, we can revisit *The Greedy Goat* when thinking about story structure—beginning, middle, and end—and model how to fill in a graphic organizer with those categories. We might read the book again to fill out a character web or to demonstrate writing a newspaper article about the event.

Because we did not have multiple copies of the book, I typed up and made several copies of the text to use for Readers Theatre. Books with a lot of dialogue work best for Readers Theatre, in which students hold the text and read the parts of the characters.

## Modeling Inference

Poetry provides a quick and interesting way to demonstrate important reading strategies such as inference. The succinct text is convenient for minilessons, and poems are sophisticated enough to be appropriate at any reading level. Flip through some poetry books and you will find poems to teach many skills and strategies. They can be written on charts or copied on overhead transparencies. One poem I use for teaching inference is "Maple Shoot in a Pumpkin Patch" (George, 1998). If it is the right season of the year, I introduce the poem with maple seeds in my hand. I read,

> Remember me?
> I helicoptered past
> your window last fall,
> then hovered over the pumpkin patch.
>
> I had traveled far on the wind that day,
> spinning the whole entire way.
> I really hadn't planned to stay,
> only wanted to look around,
> lay my dizziness down,
> rest a moment on the ground.
> No wind came to carry me aloft,
> the dirt was sweet and soft—
> I guess
> I must
> have
> dozed
> off....

Students must infer what is happening at the end of this poem. They have to use their prior knowledge about seeds and soil and clues in the poem to figure out what happened to this seed in the pumpkin patch. For an additional clue, the picture in the book can be shown, but I like to show it after our discussion to confirm our ideas. When I demonstrate with the seeds how they "helicopter" to the ground, I can pretty much guarantee that students who previously stepped on seeds unknowingly as they walked home from school will notice them now. While some students take turns releasing the seeds to watch them spin, others chorally read the poem, with more students joining in each time, learning how to read with suitable fluency and phrasing.

When we work with heterogeneous groups of students, we often find that it is the same few who participate. Our struggling learners often remain silent. Here is one way to involve all students in making meaning and conversation about inference:

1. The teacher quickly partners two students who are sitting near each other. (I might pair a child with learning disabilities with a general education student.)

2. The teacher asks, "What do you think happened in this poem?" and the partners talk together.

3. The teacher moves around and listens to the children.

4. After a few minutes, students report what their partner said to the whole group.

Students with disabilities who might not feel secure enough to volunteer their own ideas to the whole class feel comfortable in a paired conversation. First, they realize that they can safely volunteer their partner's thoughts, and soon they feel comfortable volunteering their own opinions. When we occasionally structure discussions this way, all students are talking.

If I intend to call on specific students I know will have difficulty responding, I tell them during the partner sharing that I will be calling on them. Then I listen to their conversation so I can offer assistance if necessary. As hesitant students gain confidence in speaking in front of the class, they gain confidence in themselves as learners. We might practice using inference during shared reading for several days using various genres that will be available for rereading during independent reading. I also might focus on inference during guided reading. Students with disabilities benefit from immersion in one strategy before moving on to another.

## Modeling Visualization

Another comprehension strategy is visualization, creating pictures in our minds. When we visualize, we are in fact inferring, but with mental images rather than words and thought. Visualizing and inferring are "first cousins, the offspring of connecting and questioning. Hand in hand, they enhance understanding" (Harvey & Goudvis, 2000). Katherine Lee Bates stood at the summit of Pikes Peak and captured its beauty when she wrote the poem "America, the Beautiful." Later Samuel A. Ward set the poem to music. During the War of 1812, Francis Scott Key was sent aboard a British ship to negotiate the release of a U.S. prisoner. Key overheard the admiral boasting that the American flag over the fort would not be there by morning. Key's poem, now the U.S. national anthem, tells how he listened to the sounds of battle and how grateful he felt when the flag was still visible at dawn. Both authors used visualization to write these poems, which are now a part of the American heritage.

When struggling readers are reading fluently but not for meaning, teach them to use visualization as a strategy. They will linger longer over the words if they are asked to read, picture what the author is saying, and choose a paragraph or page to illustrate. They will begin to read and think about the details in a new way.

Recently I was leading a poetry workshop in a local library. The children who signed up were third graders through sixth graders. I read six short poems to them, ancient poems by Japanese and Korean poets in the forms of tanka and sijo—forms that predate haiku (Baron, 1968, 1974). As I read the poems the first time, I asked the children to listen and picture the setting. I handed out copies of the poems and we read them together. After the second reading, I asked them to choose one of the poems and begin to draw. The beauty of these poems slipped into the students as easily as their crayons slid across the paper (see Figure 27 for Julie's visualization of

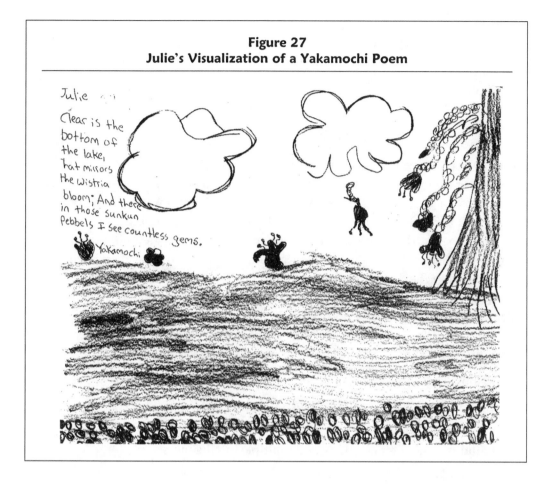

**Figure 27**
**Julie's Visualization of a Yakamochi Poem**

Julie

Clear is the
bottom of
the lake,
that mirrors
the Wistria
bloom; And there
in those sunken
Pebbels I see countless gems.

Yakamochi

a Yakamochi poem). What is so interesting about this activity is how appreciative students are of all their peers' interpretations.

Readers of poetry become writers of poetry. Some of the students in my workshop were experienced in writing, while others clearly were not. However, after the drawing activity, everyone wanted to write, and they left with a self-written poem that day.

## Visualization in the Content Areas

**Social studies: The American Southwest.**   Using poetry for choral reading will help students visualize other cultures and areas, as well as instill a love of words. To begin a study of the Southwest, I write a poem on a chart from Marcia Keegan's book *Mother Earth Father Sky: Pueblo and Navajo Indians of the Southwest* (1993) that combines poetry and photography, such as,

May my house be in harmony
From my head, may it be happy
To my feet, may it be happy
Where I lie, may it be happy
All above me, may it be happy
All around me, may it be happy.

(Navajo)

I read the poem once and I ask the class what ideas they have for reading this poem chorally. For example, do they see some lines that could be read by one person while others call for a group voice? Students suggest several different ways and we try them.

Next, I form heterogeneous groups of four or five students and I give each group two poems. They decide which poem to read and how they will present it to the rest of the class. As students make decisions about how to read their poem, they are immersed in the descriptive language of it. I allot about 10 minutes to prepare and walk from group to group, facilitating as needed. Because students are collaborating, this becomes a no-risk performance. After each group reads, classmates provide positive feedback, highlighting the various approaches used.

Why is choral reading important in inclusive classrooms?

- Choral reading fosters a love of the material, in this case, poetry.
- Rereading helps students become fluent.
- Choral reading promotes a sense of community among diversity.
- Students use their creativity and multiple intelligences.
- Students are making decisions together—an important skill for all students but a difficult one for some. They are learning how to compromise, take turns, share responsibilities, and manage time.
- Choral reading is an effective way to have shared reading experiences.

Teamwork is a necessary component in education, and choral reading of poetry lays the foundation for more complex group work such as story theater, Readers Theatre, and collaborative projects in science and social studies.

Poetry has often been the key in interesting students with disabilities in reading for pleasure. In the poetry book *I'm in Charge of Celebrations* (1986), Byrd Baylor writes about looking around her in the Southwest, in a way that allows students to visualize the small events she wants to remember the rest of her life. For example, she sees a triple rainbow and writes about being "halfway up a hill and standing in a drizzle of rain" and seeing a jackrabbit "standing up on his hind legs, perfectly still, looking straight at that same triple rainbow." She calls this day "Rainbow Celebration Day." She says, "last year I gave myself one hundred and eight celebrations—besides the ones that they close school for."

As we work with special needs students, really all students, we must be good kidwatchers and find little celebrations. I can still remember the day when Richard, a student with emotional disabilities in the class described earlier, began to love reading while visualizing Native American culture.

For a week, Richard and his classmates read together, immersed in browsing through books of Native American poetry. Each day some children planned a choral reading of a poem. The students were to copy several of their favorite poems for their personal poetry anthologies and then share at our book discussion.

Up to this point in the year, Richard had started most assignments several times with adequate ideas, only to toss them out because he could not satisfy himself. This young boy rarely showed any happiness and occasionally flared up with very aggressive behavior. During our book discussion, he threw a glance my way, indicating that he did not want to be called on to participate.

When the class period was over, I asked to see his journal. Without a word he showed me 17 Native American poems, lovingly copied in perfect print. With his hands full of poetry, he smiled at me—a rare event to be sure. I smiled too and praised him quietly so as not to overwhelm, while exploding inside with celebration. For me this moment is called "Richard's Day of Many Poems."

Read poetry across content areas. Help students visualize geographical areas of study such as the prairie, rainforest, or desert. Have students illustrate some of their poems, connecting poetry with art. (See the Appendix for books that pair art with poetry.)

Books of poetry written in two languages provide a boost for bilingual and ESL students. Children who are learning English often feel behind in school. However, they gain respect and confidence when they read a poem in Spanish that others are reading in English. Some good sources of English-Spanish poetry are *Laughing Tomatoes, and Other Spring Poems* (Alarcon, 1997), *Calling the Doves* (Herrera, 1995), and *My Name is Jorge: On Both Sides of the River* (Medina, 1999).

**Science: Birds of prey.** Jill, a gifted education teacher, wanted to try inclusion, so she joined Iris and me (regular and special education) for a study of birds of prey. Jill initiated our study by having students brainstorm a list of all the birds they could think of and then try to categorize them. Iris continued with the question, "What is a bird?" Our study of birds began with what the children already knew. All students, including students with disabilities, participated comfortably. In fact, Jill, new to the class, could not identify the special education students in the class.

Before students began to research birds of prey, we wanted them to be aware of the power of language and visualization. For homework, I asked the students to observe a bird for an extended period of time, 20 to 30 minutes if possible, and take notes (see Figure 28). The next day, I read a poem I had written after observing an egret in the Everglades. We talked about my observations and I modeled for students how I

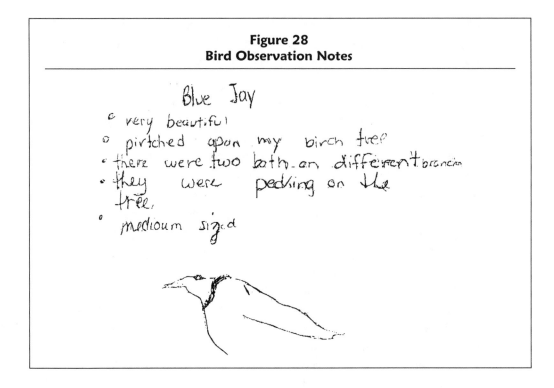

**Figure 28**
**Bird Observation Notes**

used my journal notes to write my draft. I read my final copy and then showed the students photographs of my experience. Had they been able to visualize from my words? Students, using their notes and mental images, began to write, mostly in paragraph form rather than poetry.

I asked one student if we could use her draft to demonstrate together to the class how to turn a paragraph into poetry by making line breaks and revisions. With her permission, I put her paragraph on the board (see Figure 29) and she and I discussed how poets make these decisions.

We gathered these observation poems into a poetry book and each student got a copy. Occasionally, our shared reading period consists entirely of 10 minutes of choral reading, with this student-made book of poems a favorite.

The study of birds of prey continued with read-alouds, shared and guided reading and writing, and independent activities interspersed throughout the school day. Each child chose a bird of prey to research. On some days, our shared reading was a short minilesson, reading a nonfiction article together to learn how to take notes during research on the important details of their bird. On other days our shared reading period was longer. Students decided that to safeguard their birds, they should establish a national park. Small groups of students were formed, based on their birds' habitats, and together they designed national parks across the United

---

**Figure 29**
**Student's Paragraph for Birds of Prey**

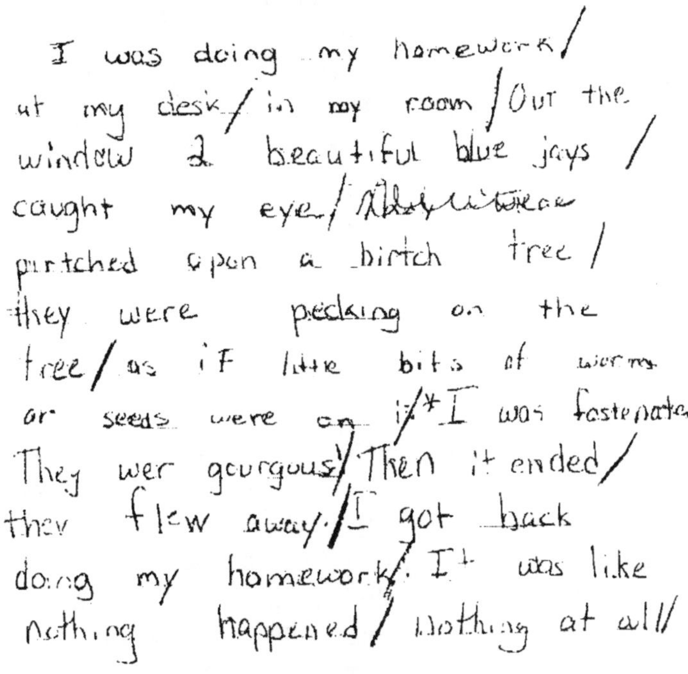

---

I was doing my homework /
at my desk / in my room / Out the
window 2 beautiful blue jays /
caught my eye / ~~they were~~
pirtched upon a birtch tree /
they were pecking on the
tree / as if little bits of worms
or seeds were on if * I was fostenated /
They wer gourgous / Then it ended /
they flew away. / I got back
doing my homework / It was like
nothing happened / Nothing at all /

---

States. Of course, they needed financial support to create a park, so during shared reading we read some persuasive essays on overhead transparencies to understand the form of persuasive writing. Several shared writing periods were devoted to writing our persuasive letters. Drafts of some of the groups' letters were made into overhead transparencies so we could think and learn together. If students with disabilities were pulled out of the classroom for services, they would not have been an integral part of the learning and fun that took place.

For the ending celebration of their work, each team gave oral presentations on their national park proposal. All students were successful. They were reading, writing, listening, and speaking. They had individual and group responsibilities, and new friendships were formed.

Although our inclusion team—Jill, Iris, and I—were all part of the planning and implementation, Jill had only 1 hour a week for inclusion, I used part of my 2 hours a day in Iris's room to support this study, and Iris managed the rest of the investigation. All students benefited from working with Jill, demystifying gifted education just as we had done with special education. We teachers benefited from this inclusion activity as much as the students, for this was definitely a joint vision, with each of us bringing different areas of expertise to the collaboration.

## *Modeling the Use of Margin Notes to Understand Text*

In *Strategies That Work: Teaching Comprehension to Enhance Understanding* (2000), Harvey and Goudvis suggest making margin notes in your own words to synthesize sections of text. Renee wanted to try this strategy with her fourth and fifth graders. We began by reading "Poem" (Hughes, 1986), written on chart paper. The poem reads as follows:

> I loved my friend,
> He went away from me.
> There's nothing more to say,
> The poem ends,
> Soft as it began –
> I loved my friend.

After reading it a few times, I asked students to underline some phrases and write what the words meant to them on the chart. Crystal underlined the words *He went away from me* and wrote *moved* on the chart while Ana wrote *He got mad at him and never talked to him again* for the same phrase. Jonathan marked *There's nothing more to say* and wrote *tragedy. The friend died.* Luis added, *He wants to cry* near the lines *The poem ends/soft as it began.* Students continued to write their interpretations on the chart, comfortable with ambiguity and interpretations.

To link our literacy learning to the New York State English Language Arts test for fourth graders, the next day we pursued writing margin notes using an article (rewritten from *The New York Times*) and a poem written by Porsha, a fifth-grade special education student in another school. Both were about the effects of global warming and the environment on polar bears. We used the format of Session 3 of the test: Students read the article and answered prompts in a graphic organizer, read the poem and answered prompts, and then organized their thinking from both pieces for a final response.

The fun and sense of challenge of using this meaning-making strategy in a shared reading experience with a Langston Hughes poem made students more confident with the test practice selections we used during shared reading. Test practice does not need to be separate from literacy. We can use authentic materials to teach the strategies students will need to reach the standards in language arts of reading, writing, listening, and speaking.

## *Modeling Reading to Find Specific Information*

Occasionally teachers want the whole class to access information from a book that may not be at the instructional level for students with special needs, such as a trade book or textbook that is central to a social studies theme. One day I was again in Jayme's room as she was helping students read about the American Revolution in multiple copies of a social studies textbook. Her objective during this shared reading activity was to teach the strategy of rereading for specific information. Most of the students' prior knowledge of the subject was limited to some of the read-alouds they had been having.

When Chall and Conard (1991) assessed students' comprehension of elementary science and social studies books, they found that only between one quarter and one half of the average-achievement students met the comprehension criteria after reading those books. They also found that only 1 of the 18 elementary science and social studies books they examined had readability levels at the grade level of intended use.

Jayme, knowing the material would be difficult, chose to use this textbook during shared reading so that all students could be assisted in accessing the information. She read a section of the text as the students followed along in their books. Then she wrote a question on a chart and students reread the section for the information needed. The students discussed their answers, articulating the same information in different ways. After the discussion, students went to their seats with their texts to write their thoughts (already rehearsed in the group) on one of the questions on adhesive notes. When they were finished, they again gathered on the rug to post their ideas on the chart and hear the different ways in which they had expressed their new knowledge in writing.

To bring the lesson to completion, the teacher asked students why it is a good idea to reread parts of text, and the students shared the following responses:

Sometimes you need certain details. (Terrell)

You need to understand what you are reading. (Michele)

To give you more information if you forgot anything. (Courtney)

If there is a part or word you don't understand you can look for context clues. (Shernay)

This information went on another chart. Notice that students' names are written after their answers to give them credit.

When material is essential to the curriculum and the reading level is much too difficult for some students with disabilities, taped books are another excellent way for students to access the reading. We must make sure, though, that students are getting the practice and instruction they need through independent and guided reading and writing activities. Some students will be eligible for taped books through the free library service at their local library or through the National Library Service for the Blind and Physically Handicapped (Library of Congress, Washington, DC 20542; Phone: 202-707-5100).

## *Modeling Word Investigations in Poetry and Prose*

There has long been conflict between advocates of skills-based and literature-based activities. Advocates of skills believe that phonics, spelling, punctuation, grammar, and other language conventions must be the focus of literacy and be taught through drill and practice. Advocates of literature-based activities think that students gain an understanding of the processes of reading and writing as they engage in meaningful activities. Students benefit from direct instruction in skills, but the skill activities in and of themselves are seldom intrinsically motivating to students. In a balanced approach to literacy, teachers teach skills in the context of whole texts, allowing students to focus on meaning. Students see the purposes of the skills when instruction grows out of meaningful literary activities (Au et al., 2001).

A student who was both dyslexic and gifted came back to see me a few years ago after graduating from college. He remembered how he had to learn vowel sounds in isolation in the early grades. He told me that even today he has trouble hearing the sounds. As he put it, "Asking me to hear the vowel sounds is like telling a colorblind person to go to the green house on the right." When he was in my class in fifth grade, instead of being pulled out of the regular class for his special education instruction, he became a part of the book discussions. He used taped books to help him keep up with his peers in the regular class. I copied short excerpts from the text for him to reread for fluency and monitored his other reading at independent levels. His motivation to practice reading came from the intellectual stimulation of the material and his dialogues with peers. He stopped resisting school and saw himself as a learner.

Duffy-Hester (1999), in a review of six research-based classroom reading programs that have been shown to enhance the reading performance of struggling readers, found that explicit teaching of word identification, comprehension, and vocabulary strategies should take place in conjunction with authentic reading and writing tasks.

Marie Clay (1998) suggests that teachers help children focus on phonemic awareness in words through enjoyable activities involving

- rhymes, poems, and songs
- stories read aloud
- rereading that emphasizes rhyme, alliteration, or segmentation of words
- manipulative activities, such as working with magnetic letters
- shared writing of messages in which the teacher asks children the sounds they hear at the beginning, middle, and end of words

Bonnie, a teacher with a love of poetry, uses a poem to launch students in an investigation of contractions. As we were co-teaching in her inclusive third-grade classroom, students gathered on the rug. She handed out copies of "I Don't Want to Live on the Moon" by poet and songwriter Jeff Moss (1989). First the class read it together to simply enjoy the thought of going to the moon, traveling under the sea, and visiting the jungle. Then they found the contractions. Bonnie charted the contraction in one column and students provided the words the contraction represents in the second column. Their investigation continued for the next several days. When students noticed contractions in their reading, they added them to the chart, placing their initials next to the addition.

On another occasion, as I was listening to students read, I noticed that many mispronounced the -ed endings in words as they read, and misspelled them in their writing. In Grade 3 and up, making generalizations about suffixes are a major focus for word study. To start our study of the suffix -ed, we read the poem "Maple Shoot in a Pumpkin Patch" (George, 1998) and listed some -ed words. Then I asked students to look around the room for more words.

The children participated eagerly, and in minutes our chart was filled with words ending in the suffix -ed. Next students discovered that -ed made different sounds, so we made categories for each word collected, such as whether the word ended with the /d/ sound, as in *played*; the /t/ sound, as in *liked*; or the /ed/ sound, as in *added*. We charted the words according to pronunciation.

Days later I asked if they noticed patterns in the spelling of words with the suffix -ed. They found these categories:

Add *ed*: grill/grilled

Change *y* to *i* and add *ed*: try/tried

Double a consonant and add *ed*: pat/patted

Drop the *e* and add *ed*: like/liked

By the end of this word study, students were able to make some generalizations about what they had discovered and wrote these in their notebooks.

In a fifth-grade classroom, we were studying the suffix -ing. Students read from a transparency of "Riding the Subway Train" (De Fina, 1997) for that minilesson. Later that day, the teacher and students could not wait to tell me how many words they were finding and categorizing, and that two boys, one of whom was a struggling student, had written and decorated an -ing poem (see Figure 30).

## Learning New Words

The purpose of spelling is so that others can read your writing. In *Spelling K–8: Planning and Teaching*, Diane Snowball and Faye Bolton (1999) show teachers the way to involve students in exciting investigations of words. They suggest teachers look at the work of students, notice common mistakes, and explore them with the

**Figure 30**
*-ing* Poem

*Christmas Joy*
*Getting up early in the morning drifting into the*
*livingroom like the water.*
*Hounding your sister and brother away, thinking about*
*what you have for Christmas.*
*Hearing all the Christmas songs jinggling in your ears.*
*Smelling the food for Christmas night.*
*Walking all around the house, talking and playing with joy.*
*Racing to get the first gift.*
*Laughing with joy.*
*Jumping up and down because of the presents you got.*
*When the snow comes down it looks like white*
*sparkling bells that shine.*
*I like Christmas, it is about giving and hoping.*

children. Whenever I see that students need to explore a particular skill, I refer to this book for guidance in structuring the lesson.

It takes time to investigate patterns, sounds, prefixes, and suffixes with students. However, when children explore and make generalizations about their discoveries during shared reading and writing, they are more invested in word study.

# Helping Readers Learn About Literary Elements

## Modeling Descriptive Language

There are many ways to help students notice descriptive language. While reading a shared text, ask students to respond by marking favorite sentences and passages with adhesive notes or copying them in a journal. These passages are interesting to share. When one student reads, other students nod in agreement—maybe they had chosen that passage too. Other times, a selection is read and students ask, "Where did you find that? That is great!" Then we flip through our books to find the words we love and missed. This inspires careful reading.

Students reread to find favorite passages, which helps memory and comprehension. At the same time, looking closely at authors' techniques and descriptive language helps us as writers. Language has the power to stop the flow of our eyes across a page and make us linger.

In my personal reading, I often see passages I want to be able to find again. Although marking the passage is one possibility, I prefer to have a journal only for excerpts. Now I can instantly retrieve a passage from a novel or lead from a feature article in the newspaper. Teachers can create a class journal in which students share a favorite passage, complete with book name and author. The class journal is a great resource for children looking for new books, new authors, and new genres to read.

## Modeling Description With Articles

During a recent conversation about models of good writing, Madalene Potter, principal of a public school in New York City, recommended that I read the writing of Selena Roberts in the sports section of *The New York Times*. Now I am hooked on the sports section and have another resource for read-alouds and shared reading and writing in the classroom. Following is an example of Roberts's writing, from the April 27, 2000, edition:

> With 14 seconds on the clock, it was Sprewell with the ball. As he waited for the clock to spin down to 9 seconds, Sprewell darted from the left sideline into the center of the paint, rose up over Carter and hit a fallaway 6-footer with 7.9 seconds on the clock to give the Knicks a 1-point lead, their first edge since the opening minutes of Game 2.... In an instant, the *Knicks were using the court as their private dance floor after winning*, 84–83. (italics added on descriptive writing)

Daily I cut out examples of good writing from the newspaper—good leads, a phrase that one can visualize, or an interesting choice of words. I use overhead transparencies so that we can read, talk about the headlines, and see how the leads pull us into an article. We even find metaphors in Roberts's tennis reporting:

The slingshot serve from the hulking Mark Philippoussis crashed into the top of the net, *ricocheting into the air on a flight as unpredictable as a paper airplane's*. (*The New York Times*, September 3, 2000, italics added)

These articles or excerpts are short enough for struggling readers to process slowly, as often as they would like. Furthermore, they often inspire sports-minded students to do more writing.

The following poem was written by Shane long before I had discovered Selena Roberts's columns. He was a special education student who was supported in inclusive classes for several years, for a while with a one-on-one assistant. Shane loved listening to sportscasters and watching games. Over time, he became so interested in writing and in meeting other children that he signed up for a summer poetry workshop, which is where he wrote this poem.

### New York Knicks vs. Orlando Magics

The game is tied at 80
when Penny Hardaway
on the Orlando Magics
gets the rebound off
the Patrick Ewing miss,
dribbles it down court and
gets fouled by John Starks.
So Penny goes to the
free throw line
with 2 ticks on the clock,
dribbles the ball 3 times,
takes a 2 second breath
since it's 2 seconds left
and he was about to hesitate
but then he remembered
his coach told him not to.
The ball left his hands
and started to roll
all around the rim.
The ball
dropped in
and at the same time
the crowd
jumped up
as high as they can.
The Orlando Magics won.

How I wish I could show him Roberts's articles and bolster his budding talent as a sportswriter.

Use articles, maps, and graphs from the newspaper for shared reading material. If you don't have copies for students, then make overhead transparencies. Use *Time for Kids* and other classroom magazines as sources for shared reading. In this way, I have used shared reading to understand the statistics on a graph of the top-selling vehicles and to read a map to find out where drought is having the most impact. We study diagrams of the dams that are impeding salmon journeys upstream to spawn and then read both points of view on the problem.

## *Modeling Theme*

Discerning the themes in a novel involves inference. The themes are the underlying ideas, morals, and lessons that give the story its texture, depth, and meaning, and are rarely written out in the story but must be inferred or felt (Harvey & Goudvis, 2000).

When I was a student, we learned silently. Work was assigned and then we read it, wrote about it, and handed it in. You were either right or wrong, and your returned paper had a grade and some comments in red. Teaching has changed. How much more fun it is to learn by listening to others and sharing perspectives.

In one sixth-grade inclusive classroom, the students were reading multiple copies of *Sounder* (Armstong, 1969) to practice discerning the themes in the book. Those who could not read the book comfortably were listening to a taped book or reading with a peer in school. As we read the novel, students discussed, reread, and reflected on their notes to discover the main themes. We created a list of themes on the chalkboard, and students realized the important themes running through *Sounder* and how many ways there are in which to say them. This is their list:

| | |
|---|---|
| Racism | Family |
| Prejudice | Determination |
| Responsibility | Hope |
| Injustice | Optimism |
| Love | Friendship |
| Bravery | Achieving dreams |
| Courage | Education |
| Strength | Religion |
| Confidence | Freedom |

When we single out a theme to assign for writing, students' work has a similarity to it. However, when students are encouraged to discuss a book and look at themes from a variety of perspectives, their writing contains a richer display of ideas, and individual voices begin to shine through.

## *Modeling Character*

Read-alouds often lead to shared reading activities, and the resulting discussion sometimes turns into a writing assignment. When I was working in an inclusive classroom of fourth and fifth graders, the teacher, Joanne, read aloud *My Brother Sam Is Dead* (Collier & Collier, 1989). After the read-aloud one day, she facilitated a discussion about the character Sam. I started a character web on a chart, and a student suggested that I write that Sam is brave and courageous because he joins the Rebels. Another student disagreed about his being courageous, and felt that Sam is dishonest because he steals his father's gun. As the conversation continued, students began to reread parts (from multiple copies) to make a point. Some students decided that Sam is a follower because he followed his friends who were joining the Rebel forces, while others decided he is definitely not a follower because he went against his father, who was a Tory. The character map grew in response to the students' thoughts (see Figure 31). Joanne and I then asked the students to look at the web and think about how they would start their paragraphs about Sam. They told us their lead sentences before they returned to their tables to write. Some of the leads in their drafts included

> "Sam is very complicated."
> "Sam is struggling with life's decisions."
> "Sam is a follower and not a follower."
> "Sam is a very confusing man."

Asking students to give us lead sentences is a great way to get students started, which is often the hardest part for struggling writers. Once they have their lead or introductory sentence, they can reread to support it with evidence.

We can also help students think and talk about character without reading an entire novel. The day I discovered Karen Hesse's book *Out of the Dust* (1999), I sat at the kitchen table and read it from start to finish. A Newbery Medal book, it is written entirely as journal entries, in poetry. The novel spans 2 years in the Oklahoma dust bowl during the Great Depression. To initiate our discussion about character, I used an overhead transparency of "Not Too Much to Ask," a poem about the mother in a family hard hit by drought. I asked students to think about this woman's character as we read the poem. From just a few words students learned how the mother handles hardships and poverty with generosity. One student remarked that they must be poor, because she made her baby a nightgown from a feed sack. Another commented on her generosity, noting how she gave away three jars of applesauce and some cured pork. They had not had a good crop in 3 years, so food must have been scarce. After this discussion, they practiced discerning character in their guided reading books by taking notes on the details that provided further insight.

**Figure 31**
**Web for *My Brother Sam Is Dead***

Students tell me that the storytelling that teachers do from their own lives make subjects interesting and important to them, so sometimes I use my own writing to demonstrate a strategy. One year, as we were studying character, my father turned 80. As a birthday present, I wrote some vignettes about him. I read a few of these stories to the students to see what they would discover about my father's character. I read about driving to Lake Michigan to see the sunset and looking for Petosky stones, fossil reminders of what was once an inland sea. I read about going to the ice cream store by way of the best place to see deer, about Dad making stilts for my children and how the whole neighborhood came over to try them, and how he packed our car for the return trip home from Michigan with tomatoes and rhubarb from the garden and a newly refinished antique chair from his workshop.

The students were accustomed to giving positive feedback, so they told me which vignettes they liked best and why. Then they asked me what he said when he got the present. I told them, "He looked at it, said, 'Ummm,' and passed it around the dining room table for everyone else to see." My students were surprised: "That is all?" I then explained that the next morning, Mom told me that Dad had taken the book to bed to read, adding, "I want one for my 80th birthday."

As we talked more about character, the students figured out a lot about my father from the stories. Soon they were able to move past words such as *nice* and *kind* to more revealing ones like *creative, patient,* and *loving.*

Something interesting happened after that family storytelling. Hannah decided to write a book of vignettes titled *Me and You, Friends.* She dedicated the book to her younger sister, Maggie, whom she called "more than a sister." Lauren made a birthday book for her older brother with vignettes about hide-and-seek, silent walks, making breakfast together for their parents, and the time he gave her some of his Halloween candy so their bags would be even. In each of the vignettes, we learned about character, and these girls were writing for pleasure.

# Conclusion

Shared reading is a vital part of the intermediate classroom. Teachers assess the needs of their students and determine what strategies to model, using a variety of nonfiction and fiction. The active participation of students during a shared reading experience benefits all students, not only students with disabilities. The use of interesting short text such as a picture book, short story, article, or poem is often beneficial in these grades. When the time used for modeling is brief, extended time can then be given for independent or small-group practice in materials of greater length.

## SUGGESTED READING

Harvey, S., & Goudvis, A. (2000). *Strategies that work: Teaching comprehension to enhance understanding.* York, ME: Stenhouse.
> Every teacher should have access to this book. Written in a user-friendly style, it consists of strategy lessons that will engage children's interests and develop their ability to make connections, ask questions, visualize and infer, and extract important information from text. An extensive bibliography to link materials to curriculum areas and areas of interest is included.

*Language Arts.* This journal is published monthly from September through April by the National Council of Teachers of English. It is for elementary teachers and has articles on literacy—strategies for the classroom as well as research and opinions.

Parkes, B. (2000). *Read it again! Revisiting shared reading.* York, ME: Stenhouse.
> This book demonstrates how shared reading helps children develop a range of strategies for reading and comprehending text. The author also discusses how to assess the teaching and learning possibilities in shared reading books and how to use a variety of text types.

*The Reading Teacher.* This journal, published eight times per year by the International Reading Association, has articles on practices, research, and trends in literacy education.

Snowball, D. (2000). *Focus on spelling* [Inservice Video Series]. York, ME: Stenhouse.
This is a series of videotapes for children in grades K–5 on learning words, exploring sounds, investigating letters and spelling patterns, and discovering generalizations. You will want to change your way of teaching word study after seeing children's excitement as they investigate words.

Snowball, D., & Bolton, F. (1999). *Spelling K–8: Planning and teaching*. York, ME: Stenhouse.
This is an invaluable resource for identifying possible spelling focuses for children at each grade level and showing how to implement class investigations into sounds, spelling patterns, suffixes, and more, always relating to the reading and writing experiences of children.

# 7

# Guided Reading and Literature Circles: Working With Small Groups

Guiding students as they read in small groups is as important in grades 3 and above as it is in the primary grades. In guided reading, the teacher meets with small groups of students, using texts that have a balance of supports and challenges, to assist students in their development of specific skills and strategies. Literature circles also are composed of small groups of students, with students choosing the books they will read and discuss together.

## Guided Reading

As Mooney (1995) notes, guided reading is the

> time when you show the children how to use resources within themselves and within the book to gain, maintain and consider meaning for themselves. Once children know how to apply and integrate the strategies of predicting, sampling and confirming text, and can regain control when meaning is lost, the focus of guided reading can shift to making children aware of how they can use these competencies to cope with more complex challenges in content and structure. These increasingly complex challenges are met in texts in content areas such as math, science and social studies, as well as in many of the books children choose to read for their own pleasure and study. (p. 75)

Our purpose during guided reading is to move students through increasingly complex text with support, so they can read the text independently. Strategies taught during guided reading include the following:

- Asking questions before, during, and after reading
- Word study
- Using meaning, structure, and graphophonic cues together

- Visualizing and creating pictures in our minds
- Making text-to-self, text-to-text, and text-to-world connections
- Retelling
- Predicting and confirming as we read
- Reading to gather details on the development of a character
- Drawing conclusions and providing supporting evidence
- Noticing the elements of nonfiction
- Locating and summarizing information
- Understanding fact and opinion
- Being able to distinguish important from unimportant details
- Determining authors' important ideas and themes
- Interpreting maps, diagrams, and time lines

In guided reading, the teacher meets with a small group of students for a particular need. The text is at students' instructional level, so with a little support, they can read it on their own and practice a strategy that has been modeled. By having a particular focus during the guided lesson, students are able to consciously implement that strategy. This leads to increased proficiency in their independent reading.

Guided reading lessons are based on the information teachers gather throughout the day—during read-alouds and shared reading and writing activities—and from running records and reading conferences with students. Teachers assess students' needs by listening to them read and by looking carefully at the writing they produce throughout the year. Teachers take notes on the needs they want to address and then form groups, ideally of four to six students, to meet that particular need. (See the planning sheet in Figure 32.)

Sometimes I teach a strategy during shared reading to the whole class and then have students practice the strategy at their instructional levels in guided reading groups. For example, I find that many of the students are not meeting reading and writing standards because they are not interacting with the text. I often use graphic organizers to help students organize their thoughts about what they have read. During shared reading, the entire class and I read and then fill out graphic organizers together. I model how to use K-W-L charts, Venn diagrams, character webs, or story maps of varying complexity as we read. Then, during guided reading, I meet with small groups of students, choosing books they can read comfortably, so that the children can practice using these organizers more independently. In this case, all the children are learning the same strategies, but they are working at the level that meets their current needs, and I am able to guide them as they practice so they can stretch even further.

---

**Figure 32**
**Guided Reading Planning Sheet**

---

Short text or book: _____

Strategy/focus: _____

Introduction: _____

Date: _____

Students and observations:

1.

2.

3.

4.

5.

6.

---

## Choosing Guided Reading Materials

In guided reading, the teacher must decide which students need a particular skill or strategy and which text they should use to practice. The text should be more challenging than their independent level but not so challenging as to be frustrating. With minimal support, students should be able to read the text the first time through and understand what has been read.

We can use a variety of materials for guided reading in the intermediate grades. Have students read newspaper and magazine articles, short stories, chapter books, and poetry. Expand their reading interests by exposing them to different genres. For example, if you are using guided reading to support word study, you might use short text such as a poem with a repeated sound or word feature. If your focus is on drawing conclusions with supporting evidence or finding the theme, longer text such as a feature article or chapter books are appropriate so that students can practice this strategy over a period of days.

If students are not reading with comprehension, find material of interest to them so they see reading as an enjoyable activity that will fill them with wonder and curiosity. Too often, special education teachers have been locked into programmed texts that do not engage the children's interest. Furthermore, such language is unnatural to the way we usually speak, making it difficult for readers to use their knowledge of syntax and semantics while they read. In *Readers and Writers With a Difference: A Holistic Approach to Teaching Learning Disabled and Remedial Students* (Rhodes & Dudley-Marling, 1988), the authors advocate choosing materials for students with disabilities that

- are written to communicate a feeling, idea, information, or story;
- use familiar and natural language;
- are relevant to the background experience of students; and
- are predictable.

Stories that work best for struggling readers during guided reading usually have repetitive or cumulative patterns, familiar story lines, a good match between the text and the illustrations, and a good match between the text and the reader's life experience and concepts. In selecting books for her guided reading collection, Sharon Taberski (2000) asks,

Will it appeal to children?

Will it motivate them to read more?

Is it attractive?

Does it convey a compelling or important message?

Is it respectful of people's differences?

Will it foster good discussion?

Does it relate to children's experience or background knowledge?

Does it present a nonstereotypical view of ethnic groups and gender roles?

## Flexible Grouping

If we group students for guided reading according to their reading level, initially it seems that the same children would be working together—the proficient readers together and the disabled readers together. But literacy is characterized by several abilities.

Opitz (1998) describes *ability grouping* as the placement of students according to similar levels of intelligence or achievement in some skill or subject, and *flexible grouping* as the placement of students in mixed groups depending on the goal of the learning task at hand. Ability grouping looks at overall reading achievement whereas a flexible group might meet to learn a skill and then the group dissolves. Some of Opitz's findings about flexible grouping include the following:

- All learners feel cared about and care about each other.

- Smaller, flexible groups make student participation more likely.

- Students interact with others in the class that they would not have otherwise.

- Interest is a major contributing factor in learning to read. Children often read at a level that surpasses their normal level when they read about a topic of interest. Groups formed on interest engage students.

On the other hand, Opitz observes that students in low ability groupings see themselves as low and perform according to their expectations, and often have isolated skill instruction rather than being immersed in language activities.

Whenever possible, students like to be flexibly grouped. It establishes the class as a community of learners. Students accept the fact that sometimes we work in leveled books, but they also know there will be times when we are learning together, regardless of level. Students at risk and students with disabilities feel much more empowered as learners in classrooms where flexible grouping is practiced. During read-alouds and shared reading lessons, students who are struggling benefit from the thinking that goes on among peers, so it also makes sense to have flexibility in our grouping for literature discussions.

Before I worked as an inclusion teacher, I pulled my students with special needs out of their classrooms for reading instruction and practice, in fairly homogeneous groups. The students made slow and steady progress. Once my students with disabilities stayed in the regular classroom for literacy activities, they worked primarily in heterogeneous groups, sometimes at a level well beyond their instructional level, with support from taped books or partner reading. They were reading above level and making more progress than I had witnessed in 20 years of teaching. Motivation from being a part of this heterogeneous setting seemed to have the biggest effect on reading progress.

## Guided Reading Lessons

During the lesson, the teacher briefly introduces the text to the students, lets them know the strategy they will be using, and supports the children as needed while they read the book, poem, or article by themselves. Discussion of the material follows and children talk about how the strategy will help them with their reading.

During guided reading, teachers have the opportunity to closely assess students' reading abilities and see how they solve problems as they read. Teachers will meet with the struggling readers more frequently, but these students also need plenty of time for independent reading.

Guided reading groups are determined by students' needs. A group could be formed to practice a strategy, such as questioning as we read, or for word study. Students might be in guided reading groups to explore a genre such as biography, for content area study, or to engage in an author study.

**Questioning for comprehension.**    As Harvey and Goudvis (2000) note,

> Questions are the master key to understanding. Questions clarify confusion. Questions stimulate research efforts. Questions propel us forward and take us deeper into reading.... Kids don't grow up knowing that good readers ask questions. In fact, schools often appear more interested in answers than in questions. Our students need to know that their questions matter. They need to see us asking questions as well as answering them. Asking questions engages us and keeps us reading.... When our students ask questions and search for answers, we know that they are monitoring comprehension and interacting with the text to construct meaning, which is exactly what we hope for in developing readers. (pp. 81–82)

A small group of students in Colleen's classroom were in a guided reading group reading *Journey* (MacLachlan, 1993). Colleen's focus was on student questioning. The photographs in Figure 33 show two of her guided reading charts on questioning. In Figure 33a, students used a double-sided format to chart their questions on one side and the answers to their questions as they read on the other. In Figure 33b, she used a double-sided entry format to model another kind of questioning. On one side she wrote a quote, and students wondered about its meaning on the other side. Students practiced these questioning techniques as they continued reading *Journey* on their own.

**Investigating the suffix *-tion*.**    As I was listening to students read in a fifth-grade inclusive classroom, I noticed that a few were having difficulty decoding multisyllabic words. They seemed unable to chunk parts of words, so the teacher and I planned several guided lessons on common prefixes and suffixes. In one lesson, our focus was on the suffix *-tion*. I gave each of the students a copy of the poem "Ations" from *A Light in the Attic* (Silverstein, 1981). I read the poem, which begins

> If we meet and I say, "Hi,"
> That's a salutation.
> If you ask me how I feel,
> That's consideration...

Students were already able to read most of the words in the poem, with the exception of the *-tion* words. We then began to investigate how to chunk these

## Figure 33
### Guided Reading Charts on Questioning

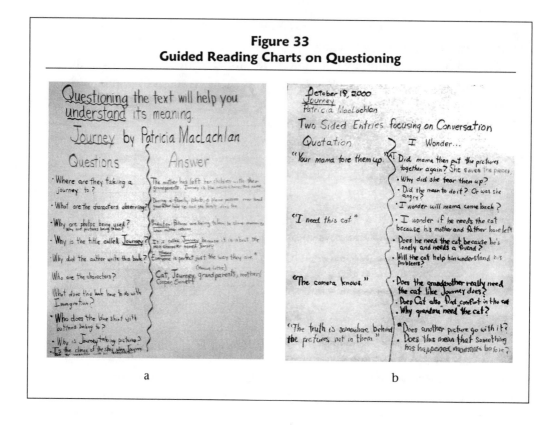

a

b

words to make them more accessible. I showed them how dictionaries chunk words and they wrote *consideration* as *con sid er ation*. They experimented with the other words, comparing their efforts. In a few minutes they were ready to read this high interest poem themselves. Their charge for the next few days was to find more *-tion* or *-ation* words and also to practice chunking multisyllabic words in their other reading.

Following this lesson, I left the room to go on to another classroom. What I did not know was that other students in the classroom overheard us reading the poem. For the next week, they all added the *-tion* words they found to a chart and surprised me with it when I came in for my next visit. Even better, students in this (low) guided reading group were being asked by their classmates for copies of their poems.

**Guided reading in a genre: Biography.** We can introduce students to different genres, such as biography, mystery, humor, or historical fiction, and find books at several levels to support students during guided reading. In a fifth-grade class, each guided reading group was reading a biography. Students were grouped according to reading level. Three special education students and two students who received support from the reading department were reading *Shark Lady* (McGovern, 1978), a book that provided the right amount of challenge for them.

The focus for all the guided reading groups was to discover important events and actions relating to their person. Students were taking double-sided notes as they read, and these notes would be used to help them write a response. The notes were set up with "Event/Action" on one side of the page and "Opinion" on the other. See Figure 34 for an example of a response to *Shark Lady*.

We are helping everyone when we use engaging multilevel materials. The students with special needs were very much a part of the classroom community because everyone was reading biographies and focusing on people of interest.

They were learning exciting information about Clark and sharks and reading at their appropriate level. They used many strategies and skills to help them understand as they read. Because this book is so interesting, the special education and at-risk students in this group were motivated to read more and many students in their classroom wanted to read the book too. These bridges between levels are

**Figure 34**
**Student's Response to *Shark Lady***

I felt good that Eugenie learned that some fish can be poisonous, and some fish can't. Eugenie said to herself "one day I would swim with a fish" and she did. I felt good at the moment when she swam with the fish. Eugenie became a doctor and married a doctor. Eugenie Clark was called Dr. Eugenie Clark. I felt good for Eugenie because it feels good to be called doctor. I felt bad for Beryl because Dr. Eugenie Clark ask him can you catch a fish?

powerful motivating factors for struggling students, making them an integral part of the learning environment. This interaction would not have taken place if the students had read *Shark Lady* as part of a pull-out program, and they would have missed the chance to realize they could read a book their peers also valued, which boosted their self-esteem.

**Guided reading and social studies: Immigration.**    Teachers in inclusive classrooms in Brooklyn, New York, were reading *In the Year of the Boar and Jackie Robinson* (Lord, 1986) as a read-aloud during a unit on immigration. This story is about a young girl coming to the United States from China at the same time that Jackie Robinson is breaking the color barrier in baseball, and the problems they both faced. This book would have been too difficult for many of the students to read on their own, but by listening to it and discussing it each day, they were able to enjoy a good book while learning about immigration and equal rights.

During shared reading and writing, fourth-grade teachers demonstrated comprehension strategies. They filled out a K-W-L chart with students to access their prior knowledge (What I *K*now) and generate questions (What I *W*ant to Know). As they found answers to their questions, they filled in "What I *L*earned." Words unique and important to the study of immigration were placed on the theme word wall so students could refer to them as they wrote. Children read from multiple copies of text and learned how to fill in Venn diagrams and take notes on important facts. Examples of these strategies were placed on the theme wall for reference (see Figure 35).

For guided reading, small groups of students read books connected to the theme of immigration. One group was reading the nonfiction book *Ellis Island* (Owens, 1998) and the other groups were reading the novel *Felita* (Mohr, 1999) and the picture book *The Whispering Cloth: A Refugee's Story* (Shea, 1996). The focus for the *Ellis Island* group was to read and take notes on the most important details. The focus for the *Felita* group was to write predictions on adhesive notes in the book as they read, and then move the note as they confirmed or adjusted their predictions. Students reading *The Whispering Cloth* were practicing a strategy on questioning. They wrote down the questions they had before they began to read and then wrote questions on adhesive notes as they read, stopping at the end of each guided reading period for a short discussion. When they finished their book, they looked at the Categorizing Questions Chart in Figure 36 (see Harvey & Goudvis, 2000). Some of their questions were answered in the text, some they could infer, and some they still wondered about. These students finished their picture book before the other groups, so they reread *The Whispering Cloth* with increased understanding, then chose from a selection of other picture books about immigration, including *Grandfather's Journey* (Say, 1993), *Halmoni and the Picnic* (Choi, 1993), *Going Home* (Bunting, 1996), and *I Was Dreaming to Come to America: Memories from the Ellis*

**Figure 35**
**Theme Wall**

Immigration ~ Journey to America

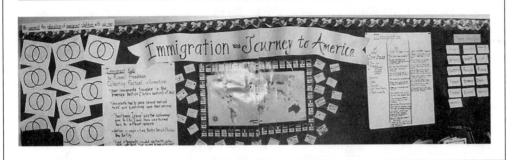

**Figure 36**
**Categorizing Questions Chart**

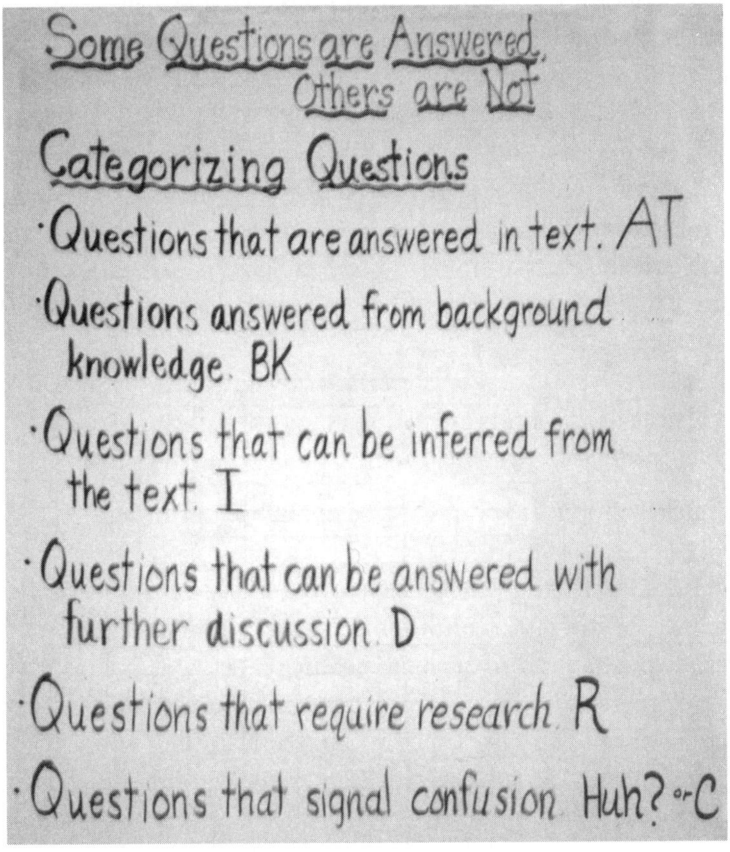

Some Questions are Answered,
Others are Not
Categorizing Questions
·Questions that are answered in text. AT
·Questions answered from background knowledge. BK
·Questions that can be inferred from the text. I
·Questions that can be answered with further discussion. D
·Questions that require research. R
·Questions that signal confusion Huh? or C

*Island Oral History Project* (Lawlor, 1997). This guided group was learning about immigration just like everyone else in the class and they recommended some of the picture books as read-alouds for the rest of the class.

Although each guided reading group did not meet daily, their notes were checked daily by the teachers. The *Whispering Cloth* group met for 10 minutes daily, the *Ellis Island* group met every other day, and the *Felita* group met every third day, a decision based on the degree of support each group needed. At the end of the books, each group wrote responses to prompts, using their notes and oral discussions to help them organize their ideas. Their final responses were scored with a rubric to help them know how they were doing in meeting literacy standards and in preparing for the statewide reading-writing assessment.

**Guided reading during research.**   Although we group students with like needs for guided reading, it is possible to find opportunities to group children of varying levels together throughout the day.

In preparation for a nonfiction study in Aimee's third-grade classroom, we read the Big Book *Meet the Octopus* (James, 1996) for shared reading. Children brainstormed what they knew about octopuses and we wrote their responses on a chart. Then we made a list of the questions we had about the octopus. As we began to read the book, we noticed features of nonfiction, such as the Table of Contents, and students looked up answers to some of their questions. They noticed bold print headings, different fonts, and how the first letter of some words was in red. They discovered diagrams with labels, as well as photographs and drawings.

Next students met in guided groups of mixed reading levels to investigate other books for features of nonfiction text. Students talked about the features they found in their small groups, wrote them on adhesive notes, and came together for a whole-class share.

The next day, when we read *Meet the Octopus* again, we asked students to think about which facts they found interesting or surprising. We modeled how to use bulleted notes to organize the information.

• The giant octopus is about the size of a school bus.

Students returned to their mixed level guided reading groups to practice reading and taking notes of interest in multiple copies of *Meet the Octopus*.

Students now had information about the organization of nonfiction text and a strategy for taking notes. Aimee wanted her class to investigate insects and asked each student to choose an insect they wanted to learn more about. Finding books to support their inquiry at appropriate reading levels was difficult; however, students used what they knew about the structure of nonfiction to help them find interesting facts, and Aimee and I supported children with their reading. Students also helped one another find and read the information they needed. When children saw information on another student's insect, they readily shared their books.

Aimee had been reading the poems in *Insectlopedia* (Florian, 1998) for her read-alouds. We used this book to model how the author embedded nonfiction information into poems. Students noticed that some of the poetry was from the insect's point of view and that Florian often used surprising facts in his poems. Students had fun as readers and researchers, becoming termites, army ants, whirligig beetles, and walking sticks.

Tatiana wrote with facts and imagination from the monarch butterfly's point of view. She began by taking bulleted notes:

- The monarch butterfly has orange and black colors. The color warns that the butterful [sic] is bitter and poisonous.

- The monarch butterfly get its poison from a plant called milkweed. It feeds on this plant when it is a caterpillar. The caterpillar shows warning color too, and is also poisonous.

- Butterfly and moth eggs are hard to see they are about the size of the head of a pin. Butterflys and moths lay large numbers of eggs on twigs, leaves, or on the ground....

Tatiana was fascinated by the second bullet of information about the milkweed plant. After writing a draft paragraph and determining where her line breaks would occur, Tatiana wrote the poem "Butterfly":

When I am
a caterpillar...
I go to
a plant
called Milkweed.
That is
where I get
my poison!
So when I am
a monarch butterfly,
birds don't
eat me...
birds don't
eat me!!!

Aimee's students investigated the features of nonfiction during both whole-class and small-group activities. The collegiality that occurs when students work in flexible and changing groups about exciting topics of interest ensures that all children get the support they need to be successful. The students' bound book of poems is now a part of Aimee's class library.

**Guided reading for an author study.**   An author study is an in-depth examination of multiple works by a single author. Teachers use author studies to help students explore the craft of writing and discover how authors communicate with their readers. When an author writes across several reading levels, all students can be involved in reading books by the same author for guided reading. Each group is reading at the right level and the teacher can support students in the groups according to their needs. At the end of the reading, students can report on their book to the whole class. In whole-class discussions, a pattern will emerge that will give students a broader view of the author than they would have from just their guided reading book. Students might fill in a chart like the one in Figure 37 to discover an author's interests and style. When students find a favorite author, they learn what to expect and books by that author become comfortable reading.

  Some authors who write across genres and/or reading levels are Cynthia Rylant (picture books, poetry, and realistic fiction), Betsy Byars (realistic fiction and memoir), Ann Cameron (historical fiction and realistic fiction), and Roald Dahl (humorous fiction and memoir). Fountas and Pinnell's leveled booklists in *Guiding Readers and Writers Grades 3–6* (2001) are helpful in finding authors that write on a range of levels.

**Figure 37**
**Author Study: Betsy Byars**

| Book | Characters | Setting | Problems | Solutions | Author's Craft |
|------|-----------|---------|----------|-----------|----------------|
| *The Midnight Fox* | | | | | |
| *The Pinballs* | | | | | |
| *Summer of the Swans* | | | | | |
| *The 18th Emergency* | | | | | |

## *What Are Other Students Doing During Guided Reading?*

Teachers need to have relevant activities available for the students who are not meeting for a guided reading lesson. How do we keep these students meaningfully occupied? The answer lies not in busywork and worksheets. Our purposes in literacy activities are to help students become better readers and writers, so they need to be reading and writing during this time. Possibilities include

- reading independently;
- reading with a partner;
- taking notes and writing responses to their reading, both in guided reading books and reading in the content area;
- reading, writing, editing, and illustrating work in progress;
- using computers for reading and writing; and
- writing on topics of their choice.

Teachers may wish to set up a writing table where students can work on their revision and editing. The area might contain lists of commonly used words, dictionaries, thesauruses, spellcheckers, paper, pencils, and pens. Students can work together quietly to help one another improve their pieces.

In addition, teachers can set up an area in the room with maps, atlases, graphs, and so forth for students to explore when their assignments are finished. Students also enjoy having a listening center available where they can listen to taped books for pleasure and think and talk together about the stories.

The best way to find meaningful activities for students during guided reading periods is to get together with several teachers to talk about what they do and what is working. The sharing of ideas is an essential part of our ongoing professional growth and makes planning much easier.

# Literature Circles

Instruction during shared and guided reading is specific and focused. Teachers choose lessons based on their assessment of the needs of their students. As students become more proficient in their reading abilities, we can introduce literature circles, also known as literature discussion groups or book clubs. In literature circles, students choose to read a book, poem, or article, and small, temporary groups of students are formed based on interest, not reading proficiency. Students have an active role in literature circles and the teacher's role moves from facilitator to occasional guide to observer.

Harvey Daniels (1994) describes the key features of literature circles:

1. Students choose their own reading materials.
2. Small temporary groups are formed, based on book choice.

3. Different groups read different books.

4. Groups meet on a regular, predictable schedule to discuss their reading.

5. Kids use written or drawn notes to guide both their reading and discussion.

6. Discussion topics come from the students.

7. Group meetings aim to be open, natural conversations about books, so personal connections, digressions, and open-ended questions are welcome.

8. In newly formed groups, students play a rotating assortment of task roles.

9. The teacher serves as a facilitator, not as group member or instructor.

10. Evaluation is by teacher observation and student self-evaluation.

11. A spirit of playfulness and fun pervades the room.

12. When books are finished, readers share with their classmates, and then new groups form around new reading choices. (p. 18)

I had read about Harvey Daniels's role sheets as an introduction to literature circle talk but I had never used them. Students in the classrooms I am a part of had taken notes and written about their reading in response journals. Then last spring I joined Linda's second grade as they temporarily left the structure of guided reading groups and tried literature circles. Linda used multiple copies of one book to introduce students to the structure of literature circles. Her students learned how to use each of four role sheets—discussion director, passage picker, word master, and artful artist. After reading a whole class novel together, students had a choice of chapter books to read and small literature circles were formed. The transformation in this room was instant and amazing. All their teacher had to say is "We're going to have literature circles now" and the students were joyfully ready. I visited this class every week and saw how empowered and serious students were with their new responsibilities and they were reading like never before. The composition of the groups was always heterogeneous and changing. Students were truly choosing what they wanted to read rather than who they wanted to read with. They loved the role sheets—just what they needed to remind them of ways to look at their reading. At the end of each book, students were very creative in deciding how to present their book to the rest of the class.

A colleague of mine says she uses the role sheets successfully all the time with her middle school students. Daniels says that this model makes it easier and safer for more kids (and more teachers) to try literature circles and I have to agree. The role sheets help create a quick, successful implementation of student-led discussion groups and once readers can successfully conduct their own wide-ranging, self-sustaining discussions, formal discussion roles may be dropped. Role sheets are temporary, meant to spark a discussion (Daniels, 1994). When I watched the Daniels video, *Looking Into Literature Circles* (2001), I was reminded of something else—during literature circles, because the talk is student initiated, there is a playful quality to it. It is a time when children can delve deeply into their reading or not;

they decide. I think it is important for us to realize that not every discussion about books has to be an in-depth analysis. We do not do that with all our personal reading, do we?

## *Preparing Students for Literature Circles*

Our work with students during read-alouds and shared and guided reading and writing activities is good preparation for the more independent format of literature circles. Students have had considerable practice talking with one another about text, taking notes, and responding to their reading in a variety of ways.

**Talk.**   Students are actively engaged in accountable talk when they discuss read-alouds and connect them to their own experiences (text to self), to other books they have read (text to text), and to the world beyond their personal experience (text to world) (Keene & Zimmerman, 1997; Wooten, 2000). Students are also talking about books when they get together to have conversations about their independent reading.

During the shared portion of the reading-writing workshop, teachers are modeling ways to respond orally and in writing. Once students are comfortable talking about their connections with their classmates, and writing about their reading, they are ready to begin book talks or literature circles. During literature circles, students talk about confusing parts that need to be clarified, connections they are making to personal experiences, and the literary elements they are noticing. When we first begin literature circles, we model what is expected and facilitate the discussions so that students can practice the kinds of open-ended discussions we are seeking. As they become more familiar with this structure, students can run their own literature circles.

**Note taking.**   During shared and guided reading and writing, we model taking notes in different ways and students practice with support. Students need experience working in different formats, and they will find ways that work best for them. Take notes using numbers, bullets, and webbing. (Third-grade students made the web shown in Figure 38 to describe the character of Amos in *Amos & Boris* [Steig, 1992].) Make double-entry columns using events/personal reflections, issues/supporting details, character trait/action (or dialogue to support it), and fact/reflection. (A fifth grader took the double-sided notes shown in Figure 39 while reading the nonfiction book *Come Back, Salmon: How a Group of Dedicated Kids Adopted Pigeon Creek and Brought It Back to Life* [Cone, 1994].) Take notes interactively during shared reading and writing and have students practice taking notes at their instructional level during guided reading and writing.

Coupling facts with reflections helps students think and wonder. It also brings their personal voices into nonfiction reading and writing. Figure 40 shows the

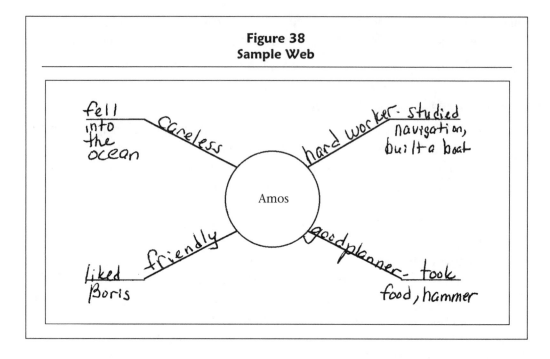

**Figure 38**
**Sample Web**

introduction to a piece written by Seth, a fifth-grade special education student in an inclusive classroom. This is an excerpt from his first draft (before any teacher assistance in revision or editing), using the double-sided notes he had taken while he read a biography of Marian Anderson.

**Reader response.**   Teachers turn more of the decision making over to students as we prepare them for literature circles. Many teachers choose to prepare their class for literature circles by having the entire class read multiple copies of the same text so that they can model the structure and decision making that will support students in their increased responsibility and independence.

I generally do not have students write a response to read-alouds because my primary reason for reading aloud to students is to interest them in reading for pleasure. I emphasize oral response rather than written response. Occasionally, I do have students respond to a read-aloud of a picture book or some nonfiction text. This brief text is good for modeling how we want students to talk and respond in writing for literature circles. When a text excites connections to the children's lives, we make entries in our writer's notebooks that may turn into a writing piece.

*Picture books.*   I read *The Whispering Cloth* (Shea, 1996), a picture book about Mai, a young girl in a Thai refugee camp in the mid-1970s, to a fifth-grade class. Mai yearns to go to a land where homes are "big as mahogany trees" and wants to build

**Figure 39**
**Sample Notes Using Double-Entry Columns**

# Come Back Salmon

## Molly Cone

| Facts | Reflections |
|---|---|
| 1. A protective layer of slime covered the baby salmon. | I think that it is important to have layer of slime even though it sounds very disgusting. |
| 2. A kid stuck his finger in the fish tank and the salmon were nibbling at it. | I thought it was funny that the fish were so hungry that they didn't now the difference between food and a finger. |
| 3. A fish died and floated down to the bottom of the fish tank because the tank was so filled with fish. | I don't entirely understand how a fish can float down to the bottom. Float means that you stay above water not stay under. |
| 4. The fish weren't getting enough air in the fish tank. | I was worried that the salmon weren't going to be able to survive without enough oxygen. |
| 5. Ammonia got into the water and might make the fish die. | If the salmon died because of ammonia in the water I would say at least we tried to save them. Even though they didn't get to the stream we could always try again. |
| 6. A kid thought that he swallowed a fry. | That is disgusting. I would know if I swallowed a fry. It would feel all slimy and taste horrible. |
| 7. The fry started jumping out because there wasn't a lot of room in the tank. | If there weren't a lot of room left I would either get a bigger tank or hurry up cleaning the stream. |
| 8. It was time to let the salmon free and back into Pigeon Creek. | I would feel bad that we had to let them go after everything we've done. It would be good for the salmon though, to live the life they were supposed to. |

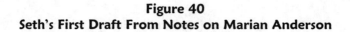

**Figure 40**
**Seth's First Draft From Notes on Marian Anderson**

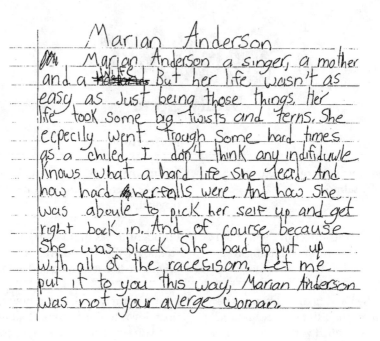

Marian Anderson

Marian Anderson a singer, a mother and a writer. But her life wasn't as easy as just being those things. Her life took some big twists and ferns. She ecpecily went trough some hard times as a chiled. I don't think any indifiduwle knows what a hard life she lead. And how hard her falls were. And how she was aboule to pick her self up and get right back in. And of course because she was black she had to put up with all of the racesisom. Let me put it to you this way, Marian Anderson was not your averge woman.

"men with white crystals" with her cousins. The following are excerpts from students' responses. They made text-to-self, text-to-text, and text-to-world connections that reach to the essence of the book.

> I think it was very smart of Mai to not give away the Pa'ndau because it was a very special thing to her. Sometimes when I craft something myself, I don't want to share my time and effort. Mai has even more reason to love her pa'ndau. She let out her past and hopes in her cloth that whispered back to her when she rubbed her face against the cloth.

> This book reminds me of *Sweet Clara and the Freedom Quilt* (Hopkinson, 1995). It reminds me of this book because in both, the girls were learning to stitch and both girls were escaping from a war or slavery. Clara and Mai ended up making something special. Mai made a pa'ndau to make money to get out of the camp to freedom and Clara made her quilt to help her and others find their way to freedom.

> Stitch by stitch, memory by memory is the way I would put Mai's pa'ndau. The roughness of her father's chin, the softness of her mother's cheek, she not only felt on her face but in her heart as a memory. Mai's grandmother was not only wise, but to me very sly. She saw the pa'ndau was not through—hope to me was the missing

link of Mai's pa'ndau. She stitched the past but was not through. Hope would make
Mai's pa'ndau through.

I liked this story a lot. I think that the artwork went well with the story. I was glad
for the little girl, Mai. I think it was good that she could stitch so well. I can
understand just how Mai felt. I have dreams for the future just like Mai.

All the students responded in important ways to the read-aloud. Each response
when shared brings deeper meaning to the book. Each response also tells us more
about that student. The last excerpt has stayed with me always. It is by a special
education student, a selective mute, and I never think of her without thinking of
her dreams for the future.

*Nonfiction.*   In Iris's inclusive fifth-grade classroom, we used multiple copies of *And
Then There Was One: The Mysteries of Extinction* (Facklam, 1993) to go along with our
study of environmental issues. We read the first chapter as a shared reading
experience, modeling some ways to take notes on the details that interested them.
We demonstrated how to take notes using a web and how to bullet important
information. Harvey and Goudvis (2000) suggest that note takers write *L* next to
something *learned* or * for information that *surprised* them. Students chose how they
were most comfortable taking notes. Our emphasis was on talking about their
reading and taking accurate notes because we were reading and writing nonfiction.

Students decided how much to read at a time and how often to meet for
discussion. Students chose to write a poem as a final response to the book. We read
a few nonfiction poems from *Creatures of Earth, Sea, and Sky* (Heard, 1997) and
*Sawgrass Poems* (Asch, 1996). Then we asked them to browse through all their notes,
pick a topic of interest, and highlight the facts they had, referring back to *And Then
There Was One* if they needed to verify information.

Anthony, a special education student, wrote his draft on the computer in
paragraph form. I helped him use the computer to make line breaks for his final
piece. (See Figure 41.)

Students in this class wrote about passenger pigeons, polar bears, bison,
peppered moths, and more. (See Figure 42 for Kathryn's poem on peppered moths.)
Even when students wrote about the same animal based on the same facts from the
trade book, they wrote with originality and voice. Although students wrote a final
response on just one aspect of the text, they have discussed many features and facts
during the process so their decision to write a poem on one animal or species
seemed a good choice. When students shared their poetry in our end of the book
celebration, we essentially had a poetic review of most of the book.

We bound their poems into a class booklet, and each child received a copy.
Not only did students read and reread these poems, we also referred to the
techniques used again and again in future writing.

**Figure 41**
**Anthony's Poem**

# Missing Tortoise

There once was a tortoise
the last one left.
They got killed
when the pirates were there.
Pirates looked all around
and killed the tortoise.
Now there was
no sight of the tortoise anywhere.
Don't you think it's just not fair?

*Fiction.* When Tricia's inclusive class was studying the U.S. prairie states as part of its study of North America, we read multiple copies of *My Daniel* (Conrad, 1991), a book about young children looking for dinosaur bones to help their family survive during years of drought and poor crops. Because this was a heterogeneous group, some students with disabilities were reading with partners while others were listening to the book as a read-aloud. Students decided how much text to read at a time and how to take notes; they then brought their notes to the book discussion.

As a final response to the book, the students also decided to write a poem, using their notes about an important event in the story. To prepare the students for a response in poetry, we read some poems from *Out of the Dust* (Hesse, 1999): "Broken Promise" and "Dust and Rain" about weather; "Debts" and "Rules of Dining" about dust.

Next we wrote a class poem. A student suggested a scene—finding the bones in the river—and I wrote his sentences on the board. Together students added sentences and reworked the wording. "We slide down the bank and see bones" became "We slide down the riverbank covered in mud and we see the dark gray bones, bigger than we had ever imagined, rising from the water. We have found Daniel's dinosaur."

**Figure 42**
**Kathryn's Poem**

 Peppered Moths

Black
and
White
they flutter
through the
trees,
and
glide through
the
fresh air.
Disappearing
on a tree
that
looks just like them,
Camouflage!
Loving life
the
Black Moth
is not
protected,
constantly
slithering
down  the
throat
of a bird.

As their
peaceful
life goes
on,
civilization
moves
in.
Not
just homes going
up but smoke blowing factories
too.
Brown,
white
trees turn to
black,
sooty
trees.
Good,
for the
Black Peppered Moth.
Bad
for the
White Peppered Moth.
Life
goes on.

Then we discussed where to put line breaks. There is not a right or wrong way to make line breaks. I often use an overhead and transparencies when we do line breaks so that we can try it one way and then erase and try another way. Here is the students' collaborative poem with line breaks:

We slide
down the riverbank
covered in mud
and we see
the dark gray bones,
bigger
than we had ever imagined,
rising from the water.
We have found
Daniel's dinosaur.

We place this poem on a chart as a model while students wrote their poetic responses. Christina, a special education student with comprehension and language disabilities, wrote the following poem on her own:

**Daniel's Death**

Death was coming toward Daniel,
struck by lightning he lay there,
not one sound,
not one heartbeat,
nothing.

Death was coming toward Daniel,
struck by lightning he lay there,
Julie calling,
calling his name repeatedly,
not hearing anything she stood there,
stood still until she realized,
Daniel was gone,
gone forever,
not coming back,
ever.

Death was coming toward Daniel,
struck by lightning he lay there,
lying there with only a bone in his hand,
the only thing he wanted,
the only thing he loved.
Now he's gone and so are his dreams,
all gone,
gone.

The students in Tricia's class enjoyed all the poems equally. With the recognition from peers and teachers, Christina and the other students with disabilities in this class found their voices through poetry, becoming empowered to use their intelligence and time in new ways to compensate for their disabilities.

If I had tried the same reading and poetry responses with my special education students as a pull-out group, they might have written as well but they would not have had the reinforcement of having all their general education peers love their poems. The students with special needs would have compared themselves favorably to other students with special needs, not with everyone in their grade. This makes a big difference in self-esteem and, in turn, motivation.

## Literature Circles and Student Choice

When we offer a choice of books to students, they can practice their increased autonomy in small groups. In this next example, the classroom teacher and I gave children a choice of three books—*Number the Stars* (Lowry, 1998), *Sounder* (Armstrong, 1969), and *The Cay* (Taylor, 1991)—and taped copies were available for students who could not read these books independently.

Students decided how much should be read at a time and either read alone or with a partner. Students with disabilities could comfortably join literature circles when supports such as partner reading and taped books were available. Students decided on what kind of note taking and responding would occur during the reading and set a date to meet for discussions. These discussions were rich in details. It was a time to retell, think, affirm what they understood, clarify what they did not understand, and predict what they thought might happen next.

Many students, as they read and responded, were not taking the time to organize their journal writing and edit for conventions such as punctuation and spelling. A lot of writing was being done around their reading, but students were perpetuating errors, and parents were becoming more concerned with spelling and grammar than with the sophisticated level of the thinking. To address this, we assigned a grade to the notes. The discussions and journal work became drafts to reflect on before constructing a final response that was revised and edited to the highest ability possible.

When students were writing these final responses, we set aside time for sharing our writing in progress at the beginning or end of our reading-writing periods. Because this was my scheduled inclusion time, I conferenced with all the children, although I was targeting the four special education students in the class. While some students write and rewrite to learn what they want to say, the final copies of some students would be almost the same as their original drafts if we did not intervene. Furthermore, when special needs students see all children conferencing and reworking their pieces, they become more willing to improve their drafts. With two teachers in the room for these periods, we can make sure that we conference with everyone.

Sean, a special education student with reading, attention, and memory difficulties, used a recorded book to support his reading of *The Cay*. Others overheard the tape and wanted to hear the story, complete with dialects, so they joined Sean in "reading by tape" for a few chapters.

Sean originally started his response to *The Cay* as follows:

> Phillip is on a boat that is torpedoed and hits his head. He is mad at the black man on the raft.

However, after listening to some of his classmates' work, he asked to have a conference with me. By responding to my open-ended questions, he expanded his ideas. Part of general education and special education teachers' responsibilities in inclusive classrooms is to learn how to ask good open-ended questions that encourage talk. Sean, as well as other students not in special education, need to have conversations before they write. His rewrite appears in Figure 43.

Although Sean had difficulty with miscues and comprehension, he was learning how to retell the story. By listening during student discussions, he was able to make higher level connections to the text. Avoidance of schoolwork gradually was replaced by increasing lengths of time spent on task. After being in a full day self-contained program for several years, he was proud to be a part of the regular class, and he rehearsed his written response several times so he would be able to read or talk about it with fluency to the group.

When Sean shared his responses in his literature circle, he was complimented on his ideas and received positive peer support. Although he had responded in writing to open-ended questions while some of his classmates wrote more independently, they had all achieved success in their reading and writing, and

---

**Figure 43**
**Sean's Rewrite**

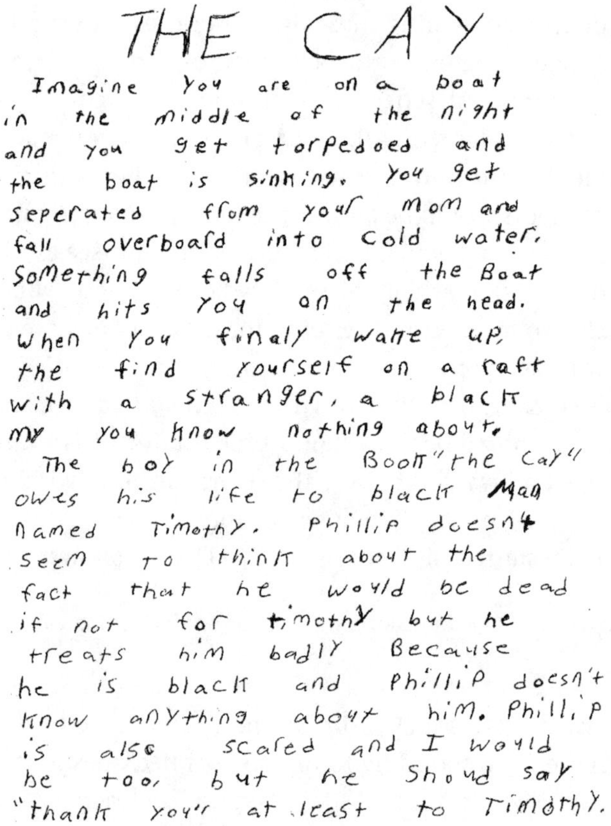

---

# THE CAY

Imagine you are on a boat in the middle of the night and you get torpedoed and the boat is sinking. You get seperated from your mom and fall overboard into cold water. Something falls off the Boat and hits you on the head. When you finaly wake up, the find yourself on a raft with a stranger, a black my you know nothing about.

The boy in the Book "The Cay" owes his life to black Man named Timothy. Phillip doesn't seem to think about the fact that he would be dead if not for timothy but he treats him badly Because he is black and Phillip doesn't know anything about him. Phillip is also scared and I would be too, but he shoud say "thank you" at least to Timothy.

gained important understandings about diversity and how it relates to their own lives. When the students in each book group listened to the perspectives of the others, they expanded their understanding of the novels and their own ability to make sense of the world.

**Varying the way we respond to books: Readers Theatre.**    Readers Theatre is a kind of oral storytelling in which literature is the focus. Students write scenes from a book to portray the various characters' points of view. Voice, facial expressions, and gestures make the characters and narration come alive. Stories with dialogue and a strong plot work best. There is an audience, but costumes, sets, and memorized lines are not necessary (Galda & Cullinan, 2002).

During an author study of Betsy Byars, students chose to read *The Summer of the Swans* (1970), *The Pinballs* (1993), or *The Midnight Fox* (1996). When we introduced the books to the students so they could choose one for their literature circle, we mentioned that in each story there are young children who are struggling with some problems and gave information about setting and characters. Students selected the book they wanted to read and heterogeneous groups were formed. Each group decided how they would schedule their reading, how they would take notes, and how often they would meet to discuss their reading. For example, one group decided to meet two times a week and to put adhesive notes on critical events in the story. When all the groups finished with their books, we brainstormed possible ways in which they could respond. Students suggested drawing, writing a response, writing about how a character changed from the beginning of the story to the end, and acting out a part of the story. We explained Readers Theatre to them to see if that would be an option they would like and they did.

Children love the opportunity to act out scenes in Readers Theatre. When they use their imaginations to respond to literature, they not only flourish but they spend more time on their work—often with astounding results.

One of the interesting things about using Readers Theatre as a response to literature is the changing group dynamics. In this classroom, the student who was a selective mute chose to take the talking role of a sister. The student who struggled most with writing conventions (such as spelling) and organizational skills took the leadership role in writing the script and organizing the group for *The Summer of the Swans*. The script was written, lost, and rewritten quickly, but no one mentioned this as they practiced for their performance. Here is part of the script:

### The Summer of the Swans

| | |
|---|---|
| Narrator: | Joe and Sara are looking for Charlie like a hawk looking for its pray. |
| Sara: | Charlieeeeeeee!!!!!!! charlieeeeee!!!!!!!!! |
| Joe: | It's no use Sara he is no where to be found. |
| Sara: | We have to keep looking he's my brother, charlieeeeee!!!!!! |

| Narrator: | suddenly Sara here's a formilyore screech from the reiven that could only be her brother. |
|---|---|
| Sara: | It's Charlie, Joe it's Charlie!!!!!! |
| Narrator: | Sara rases down the hill with dirt and dust flying behind her dispite that the one thought in her head is to get to Charlie. |
| Joe: | are you sure? Sara wait up! |

Their script calls for the sister and the aunt to hug the lost brother. The preadolescent classmates were not sure they wanted to hug, but they discussed it and decided that it was crucial to the story of family relationships. Their classmates applauded and gave positive feedback, explaining that they could understand how the family feels because the group showed it through their conversation and hugs.

Three students in *The Midnight Fox* group wrote six scenes, and they brought an animal cage to school as a prop for the captured baby fox. The student with disabilities in this group had the lead, a quiet underachiever took the part of two characters, and the student who was pulled out for the gifted program chose to be the baby fox, a nonspeaking role in which she simply sat in the cage whining for her mother. Here is part of their script:

**The Midnight Fox**

Part 1

| Narrator: | Tom is a city boy. His parents made him go to his aunt's farm. Tom hates it until... |
|---|---|
| Black fox: | (Walk around and lift head up every now and then. Sniff the grass.) |
| Tom: | (Write fake letter to Petie and look up occasionally.) There's nothing to do. I'm so bored. All I do every day is sit around and wait for a letter from Petie. Wait, what is that creature on the crest of the hill? It looks like a fox. |
| Narrator: | Tom looks up in amazement at his new discovery. |
| Black fox: | (Walk closer to Tom. Let out a few high pitched barks. Dash off to woods.) |
| Narrator: | And this was the beginning to Tom's adventure. |

The *Pinballs* group went off in an entirely different direction. They acted out three short scenes that were critical to understanding each main character and then presented three pinball games they had made out of clay, each game representing the characteristics of a main character.

This is what is so beneficial about varying our expectations. When we encourage a variety of responses, students are able to show talents that would lay undiscovered if all we asked for were written responses. There is camaraderie, humor, disagreement, and problem solving, all in just a few literacy periods, and then praise from peers and teachers. With limited time for preparation, students learn to use time well to focus and plan.

We asked the students to evaluate their presentations—what they contributed, what their group did really well, and what was difficult about working with a team. Noting what was most difficult, students wrote,

> At some points we kind of struggled, but then we combined them all together to perform a glorious play.
>
> Everyone has a different opinion
>
> It was hard to fit everyone's needs.
>
> It was difficult to work with each other. It is hard to not do just whatever you wanted.
>
> To me the difficult part was when we wrote the script because we had some arguments but we worked them out.

When asked what their group did really well, they responded,

> Cooperate with each other.
>
> We worked together as a team and we all participated.
>
> Teamwork, like when someone made a mistake but the other members helped that person.
>
> One thing that we really did well was we worked together and listened to our peires [sic].

Although it is critical for students with disabilities to work at their instructional level, which may be considerably below "grade level," it is during these heterogeneous activities that they often become inspired and motivated to reach for new levels and to put more time into learning activities. During Readers Theatre, students were involved in the literature and they had fun working on their scenes. Students showed unknown talents. They used problem-solving skills to overcome the hurdles, and students came away with a good feeling about themselves and their team, and with an interest in reading another Byars book, sparked by what they had seen.

**Modeling writing in the style of favorite authors.**    In Matt's inclusive classroom of fifth graders, we used *Cactus Poems* (Asch, 1998) to model how the writer used his interest and knowledge about science to write in both expository *and* poetic forms. *Cactus Poems* is a book of photographs and poetry about the desert, with endnotes in which the author adds more information about each topic in expository form.

The students had just finished reading *Come Back, Salmon* (Cone, 1994), a nonfiction photo essay about students who clean up a polluted creek so salmon can complete their life cycle there. Although the desert life in *Cactus Poems* has nothing to do with the life cycle and problems of salmon in the northwestern United States, we do not need to find materials matching in content in order to model writing structures. To prepare for our writing, which would also take the form of poems and expository material, students listened to the titles and selected desert poems for me to read aloud. We read to satisfy our curiosity, to hear the poetic language, and to notice the poetic choices Asch makes. His topics include waterless shores, bobcat watching, magic rocks (petroglyphs), and the saguaro cactus. There is variety in poetic style also—narrative poems, poems arranged in stanzas, list poems, and concrete poems where, for example, the words about the cottontail rabbit hop all over the page.

Students then wrote about the content of *Come Back, Salmon*. They wrote about litter in the creek, how elementary children can make a difference, and how baby salmon are raised. Some wrote about how salmon remember and return to their home creek to mate and complete the life cycle. Taylor, with a sense of humor, called her poem "Fry," creating this beginning:

> Not the fries you eat
> At Burger King or Mickey D's,
> I'm talking about fish.
> Another name for
> a baby fish
> is a fry.

Her expository paragraph told about the children of Jackson Elementary School and how they cleaned Pigeon Creek and then returned fry to it. To make a class book, we followed the format of *Cactus Poems*, placing poems and pictures in the beginning and the additional information in paragraph form at the end.

The children were excited to get their own copies of the class book, and they read and reread one another's poems and paragraphs. As they reread they noticed the poetic techniques that were tried and the different style in expository writing. The value of an assignment like this is that by writing only a poem and a paragraph, we have used just a few days, not weeks of time. Short assignments like this are valid and important in inclusive classrooms—manageable and successful activities for children and teachers alike.

Some of the best work I have seen in poetry is from students with the most difficulties. Because poetry does not seem like an impossibly long and overwhelming assignment, the passive and the procrastinators get their work done, with a little extra conferencing from the general education teacher or me. Although poetry may be as sophisticated in content as other types of writing, students meet success faster, merely on the small amount of words that need to be written. When they receive positive feedback from their peers, they become more motivated and do more work.

**Letting imaginations soar.**   When we vary the ways in which we allow our students to respond, we seem to inspire them even more. Not only do we bridge their learning gaps, but we also leave lasting impressions. These are the projects they keep long after the assignment is over, and these are the activities that encourage them to read and write for pleasure, act in a play, or pursue drawing outside the school day.

In another inclusive class reading *Come Back, Salmon*, we gave the students a choice of how to respond. Adrian painted a large picture of salmon and eggs, contrasting the turbulent ocean and the calmer stream. Mike, usually an underachiever although he does not have special needs, drew and cut out 15 salmon, pasting them on oak tag to show how they attempt to get past the dam on ladders and up the stream. Danny, newly skilled in PowerPoint, made a picture book. Elaine drew before-and-after illustrations of Pigeon Creek, placing a salmon in the clean stream on a stick so that we could move it through the water. She also included a diagram of the life cycle with important features, wrote about the life cycle, made a questionnaire for the class, and ended with salmon recipes from the Internet.

When we provide students with choice, they have fun with the variety of response possibilities, and praise for creativity flows in everyone's direction. In this particular classroom, all the students came away from the experience loving nonfiction and feeling that every person can make a difference in their environment. Sometimes teachers or parents question if students who excel will be challenged enough in inclusive classrooms. I have found that they are.

### Final Thoughts on Literature Circles

Our daily immersion in talk and writing about our reading during read-alouds, independent reading, and shared and guided reading and writing activities provides wonderful preparation for the student decision making required in literature circles. Students are accustomed to making connections to their reading and to discussing and broadening their perspectives with peers. Student response to reading is modeled and students respond to fiction and nonfiction in a variety of ways. Students are ready to choose books they want to read and join others with the same interest in small groups.

Literature circles are predictable, playful, and meaning-centered activities in which children exercise lots of choice and responsibility, and structures are provided that help students function at a higher level than they could unaided.

## Conclusion

Teaching is constant decision making, and I am still thinking through how to balance my focused guided reading lessons with literature circles in which books are chosen by the child based on interest. Watching children makes me believe that both are necessary parts of our small-group instruction. I want students with disabilities to get the practice they need at a level in which they need minimal support, and I want them to be excited by the prospect of choosing a book by interest and reading with ever-changing small groups of peers.

When I consider the reading we do in small groups during our literacy block, I now feel comfortable advocating for a balance between teacher-planned guided reading groups and student-directed literature circles. During guided reading lessons, teachers focus on specific needs of students. These focused lessons help students become independent in the use of strategies and knowledgeable about reading in different genres, both fiction and nonfiction. During guided reading, students meet the challenges of more complex information and longer texts. For students with disabilities, it is essential for them to have specific guidance at their instructional level. Teachers ready students for literature circles during guided reading lessons, as well as during book discussions after read-alouds and during shared reading. Literature circles are still structured, but with student choice—choice of book, how much to read, what to discuss, and how to respond. With the student decision making and camaraderie that accompany literature circles, I have seen students with disabilities soar to success. These students are an integral part of their heterogeneous class, reading what their peers also want to read; this motivates them to read for pleasure, changing them as readers and writers.

## SUGGESTED READING

Atwell, N. (Ed.). (1990). *Coming to know: Writing to learn in the intermediate grades.* Portsmouth, NH: Heinemann.
> The connections between reading and writing are explored in this book as well as journal writing, taking notes, conducting research, and the role of children's literature in teaching science, social studies, and math.

Cullinan, B.E., Scala, M.C., & Schroder, V.C. (1995). *Three voices: An invitation to poetry across the curriculum.* York, ME: Stenhouse.
> This book is organized into 33 strategies for using poetry across the curriculum, with a vignette telling how each strategy worked in the classroom and examples of student work.

Daniels, H. (1994). *Literature circles: Voice and choice in the student-centered classroom.* York, ME: Stenhouse.
> This is a good book for the beginner thinking about starting literature circles and for the experienced, wanting to think about all the possible ways to involve children in joyful reading and decision making.

Fountas, I.C., & Pinnell, G.S. (2001). *Guiding readers and writers grades 3–6: Teaching comprehension, genre, and content literacy.* Portsmouth, NH: Heinemann.
> This book explores all the components of a quality upper elementary literacy program, with special help for struggling readers and writers at the end of each section. Also included is a comprehensive booklist organized by title and level.

Harvey, S. (1998). *Nonfiction matters: Reading, writing, and research in grades 3–8.* York, ME: Stenhouse.

This is a practical and exciting resource for exploring nonfiction. Harvey advances the importance of teacher modeling and guided practice in instructional delivery, and presents strategies for understanding expository text.

Rhodes, L.K., & Dudley-Marling, C. (1988). *Readers and writers with a difference: A holistic approach to teaching learning disabled and remedial students.* Portsmouth, NH: Heinemann.

This book was written to provide teachers of students for whom literacy learning has been a struggle with a more meaningful, purposeful approach to reading and writing.

# 8

# The Opportunity to Be the Same—for Now

Each school year begins with a mixture of excitement and anxiety. Teachers, parents and children are all hoping for a successful year. Parents of students with disabilities and at-risk students may be hoping their child catches up academically, has social activities, and develops a sense of belonging with peers. Their children's hopes may be as complex as wanting to read, write, and calculate perfectly or as basic as making it through another school day. We are all in this together, hoping that the school year will make our dreams come true.

In the years that I have been working as an inclusion teacher, I have found that using a balanced literacy approach, with its beliefs on the importance of heterogeneous groupings and immersion in talk and reading and writing across the curriculum, is most instrumental in the success of both regular education students and students with disabilities.

In a study that examined third-, fourth-, and fifth-grade students' perceptions of the composition of reading groups, an overwhelming majority preferred mixed-ability grouping. They felt that all students made more progress in mixed ability groups, with the exception being nonreaders, who students perceived learned best in same-ability groups (Elbaum, Schumm, & Vaughn, 1997).

Inclusion, with its heterogeneous mix of children, has not only blurred the lines between special education and regular education, it also has clarified a too common misconception about what a learning disability really is. Before inclusion, teachers would sometimes say to me as they reminisced about a student they once had, "You wouldn't know Sara," implying that she was too capable for me to know as a special education teacher. Inclusion erases these misconceptions and teachers understand, from working closely with special education students, that a learning disability is not lowered ability but a discrepancy between the child's ability and performance.

By using a balanced approach to literacy instruction, I also became convinced that all students need to learn from interesting materials and be involved in authentic learning tasks. Students with mild to moderate disabilities learned, along with their general education peers, by listening, through conversations, and from demonstrations. They read engaging books and articles, talked about what they were reading and writing, and practiced the strategies and skills with increasing independence. Everyone was acknowledged for what they could do. Being a part of the stimulating class discussions that happen around exciting books and articles gave students with disabilities a feeling of being a learner and belonging. This motivated them to spend more time practicing reading and writing at their independent level, an important factor in their rising success rates. Both students in general education and special education made gains socially and academically. There is no reason to isolate skills and strategy work for students with disabilities from materials that engage children and authentic learning activities.

This chapter begins with a look at the progress of one student over the course of her first year in an inclusive classroom. The chapter continues with the voices of students I have worked with, highlighting how they have benefited from their placement in inclusive classrooms. It concludes with the reflections of parents—the children's first and constant teachers.

# Kristen's Progress

Throughout this book, I have been writing about the daily successes of students in inclusive programs. What does progress look like over a year's time? This section contains a more detailed discussion of Kristen, a fifth-grade special education student. She had received special education services throughout her school years, first in self-contained full-day programs and then in a pull-out program for 2 hours daily. In fifth grade she was fully included for the first time in a general education classroom, with 2 hours of special education inclusion services provided there daily.

For the past several years, she had been taught phonics and structural analysis. Her teachers also used Orton-Gillingham and Glass Analysis to assist her decoding. When asked to read a list of words in isolation, without any context, she read *friend* for *field*; *with* for *white*; *over* for *other*; *visit* for *vehicle*; *demonstration* for *departure*; and *speaks* for *spreads*. Although her reading always had some miscues, when she read for meaning in a story that provided context, she could use more than one cueing system to self-correct and meet with success.

In addition to her decoding difficulties, Kristen had a short attention span and acted impulsively. She tested in the very superior range of intelligence with a Full Scale IQ of 137 on the WISC-R. Although she had strengths in abstract reasoning ability and word usage, she showed significant weaknesses in the areas of reading, spelling, arithmetic, and fine motor coordination. On the Diagnostic Achievement Battery, she scored at the 91st percentile of story comprehension (listening) but at the 5th percentile on short passages for reading comprehension, which required decoding more than constructing meaning. This disharmony between intellectual ability and academic functioning created a great deal of frustration for her.

In spite of her learning disabilities, Kristen needed to be in an inclusive classroom. I wanted her immersed in the intellectual and social learning and literacy going on in a general education classroom. Literacy is more than decoding; it is learning from the spoken word as well as the written word. It is thinking and understanding. For her to be prepared to join some fifth-grade literature circles with her peers, we discovered many strategies that worked.

If students are to become better readers, they must read, and this often includes spending time listening to stories. When we balance the ways in which students experience books, they become better readers. However, when I first suggested that Kristen use a taped book in September, she was very resistant. Her mother wrote me a note, stating,

> She is very hard on herself. She thinks she is stupid. She insists on reading and must know every word in the reading. Homework is full of daydreaming and emotional outbursts.

Her mother and I soon learned that Kristen was opposed to using the tapes because she considered listening to a taped book cheating. Knowing this, I pointed out that listening is learning and that all students listen to learn daily, especially during read-alouds.

By October, Kristen adjusted to a mixture of using tapes, being read to, and reading on her own. Soon her mastery of the information and her contributions during discussions proved to her that she was a valuable addition to the group and that reading this way was valid. Her mother wrote,

> She "allowed" me to read every other page last night. Apparently you read to her and explained that it was okay as long as she got the idea of the story. We will be able to get through the book with much less emotional strain this way.

Kristen eventually liked the independence that learning from tapes provided so well that we ordered books through the Library of Congress for her. She followed along with the tape and I selected pages of the book for her to reread on her own. She already knew each story through listening, so she felt quite fluent when rereading the passages I chose.

I have come to believe that fluency does more for decoding than decoding does for fluency. The more Kristen listened, the more she learned and the more motivated she became. The more motivated she became, the more willing she was to reread passages and thus read more fluently. With the fluency of reading known material, her interest in the literature, and the growing confidence that came from being a valued part of the class, she started spending more time reading, and it showed.

Later that year, Kristen's class was going to read multiple-copy books of *The Lion, the Witch, and the Wardrobe* (Lewis, 1994). Her teacher planned to read part of the book as a read-aloud with accountable talk, and to assign some chapters to be read independently. Her teacher loved this book, and I wanted Kristen to be part of the fun that would ensue, even though the book was at an inappropriate level for her to be reading without support.

I also provided tapes so Kristen could listen to some of the chapters at home, and I sometimes summarized chapters with her orally so we could move ahead at the speed of the regular class. On days when the classroom teacher allotted time for reading, Kristen read together with her friend Colleen. They would sit together on a beanbag chair, with Colleen doing the reading and Kristen making connections. Together, they helped each other through the story. Kristen was empowered by being able to choose what help she wanted. Having options for reading (tapes, teachers, students, parents) gives students with disabilities a sense of control.

In addition, we tried several ways to complete written assignments, so that Kristen would have a repertoire of methods from which to choose. After we read together, she wrote a journal response by herself. It was two pages, written in large and laborious print with many misspellings. Figure 44 shows part of her response.

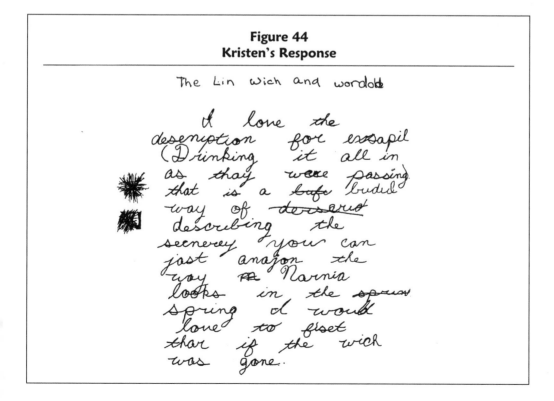

**Figure 44**
**Kristen's Response**

The Lin Wich and worldob

I love the desenption for exsapil (Drinking it all in as thay were passing that is a bafe budil way of derserut describing the seenerey you can jast anajon the way fa Narnia looks in the spwu spring I would love to fleet that if the wich was gone.

Kristen spelled *Narnia* correctly because she was able to find it on the back of the book. She could have used the same strategy to spell *witch*, but she was writing quickly to get her ideas down on paper. She sounded out words as she wrote. It is possible to hear *visit* as *fiset* when you whisper the word, which she was doing at her desk. When we read over her writing, we noticed some of the words she often used and misspelled. We made a list of these words for the back of her journal so she could easily refer to them. I also gave her a SpellWell bookmark, which contains the "100 most often misspelled words." These bookmarks are handy, easy-to-use references to help students quickly access words. They are available from Curriculum Associates, Inc. (800-225-0246).

The next time we read together, Kristen dictated a response, which she then copied into her journal. It was one and a half pages long, in smaller, neater print with conventional spellings. Kristen had a wonderful vocabulary, which she did not have the patience to try to spell, so she felt more competent with the dictated response. With a better sense of her own abilities, she participated more in the discussion group.

With dictated responses, some students with disabilities can express themselves more creatively. When they write with more creativity, they expand their reading vocabulary. They are willing to spend more time on academic tasks because the end result looks sophisticated. Although this motivation comes from within, they also receive positive feedback from peers and teachers. The strategies they develop and their growing confidence transfer into writing on their own. Gradually they become independent writers, which is continually being encouraged and expected.

Most of the time I had Kristen start a draft of her ideas and then dictate only a part to me. By starting a draft, she gained the experience of searching for ideas and putting them on paper on her own. In dictating the rest of her response, she was able to save time and practice copying with correct spelling in her journal.

Many students, not just students with disabilities, have developed habits of misspellings over the years that are hard to break. If a child misspells *said* as *siad* for even a few months, it is written incorrectly and reinforced many times. When Kristen copied the dictation, she was seeing and copying words that were spelled correctly. Again, she also articulated her ideas with a better vocabulary than when she stopped to sound out each word. She was then willing to spend more time thinking of higher level connections or trying different writing techniques, such as an engaging lead.

Dictation was also an option for homework, which takes longer for students with disabilities. Although we encourage increasing independence, the time spent on homework is a factor that means some compromise may be required. One morning, Kristen brought me a note her mother had written the night before:

> Tonight at 9 P.M. I finally let her dictate the response to me. She will copy it. When she talks the thoughts just flow. I thought you should know that she tried to do it alone and I gave up and helped her.

Whenever there was time, I expected Kristin to copy the dictation in her own handwriting or on the computer so she would have the experience of seeing her words spelled correctly. But if she was being diligent and spending more time reading independently on her just right level, I helped her save time by typing on the computer as she dictated. We would print out a copy so she could rehearse before the book discussion group met. In other words, I did not expect her to do every part of the reading-writing process on her own. I continually weaved in help at different parts of the process, so that she grew in independence in all ways—just not in all ways at once.

When Kristen wrote on the computer, her work looked entirely different. Figure 45 shows her computer-written response to a short story from *Every Living Thing* (Rylant, 1988). Rylant's story is about a boy with disabilities and his turtle. Although Kristen struggled with cursive writing, she challenged herself with a script font.

Rehearsal, a form of rereading, improves reading and speaking fluency. Many students with disabilities are able to read their computer-printed response easier than their handwriting, just as they are able to read print easier than cursive

---

**Figure 45**
**Kristen's Computer-Written Response**

---

*Slower Than The Rest*

    *I think some of the ways that Leo changed was that he had something to care about instead of feeling sorry for himself. The reason he didn't feel slower than the rest was because he knew more about Charlie than anyone else. He had someone to talk to*

    *and relate with and Charlie could not talk back to him or make fun of his problems, and that's what made him such a good friend. Charlie made him feel important because he helped Leo win the contest. Also, Leo with Charlie's help learned that being himself was A-okay!!!*

writing. Although it is important for students to have opportunities to read print in different forms, for some students this is an "unseen" problem. I once had a boy with reading disabilities start to cry when taking a test in the general education classroom. When I questioned him, it was not the content that was upsetting him but the fact that the test had been typed entirely in capitals, which looked like a different language for him.

When Kristen discussed her ideas during book discussions, her classmates were quick to agree with her statements and comment on the details she chose. She was a part of the intellectual mainstream and respected for her views, which gave her the courage and stamina to continue working on the reading and writing process.

By February, Kristen was joining new groups of students for her guided reading sessions. She was reading historical fiction, books that interested her, for her independent reading. She was spending much more time on homework and requested tapes only for nights when she had a lot of homework in other subjects or other obligations to meet.

Kristen stopped using taped books completely in the spring. It took her longer than most of her peers to read assignments, but she was proud of being able to do it. When she was not able to finish her reading and writing on time, she did not avoid the task. She would leave a note on my desk asking for help that day. She was advocating for herself now.

Socially, things were changing, too. Whereas her mother's notes used to worry about teasing on the bus and the playground, she now wrote,

> I have good news. She goes out to play after school in the neighborhood.

Within a year, Kristen was reading on her own without tapes. The power of knowledge, curiosity, and respect from peers, teachers, and parents helped her become more tolerant of her miscues, which were happening with much less frequency. Her mother reported,

> She did her "book talk" homework tonight with no help. She also did all the reading this week alone. Yesterday Crystal and Brianna came over! Such socializing.... By the way, she wants to be a writer.

It is not easy being the parent of a child with disabilities. The excerpts shown here were only a small part of the communication I had with Kristen's mother. She was concerned, frustrated, and honest. Because of her willingness to work with me, I had a better understanding of her child, and we were able to ease Kristen into regular activities without undue stress. When Kristen saw all her classmates using the same strategies she was using, she was less anxious. When she was sought after for her insightful contributions, she gave up some of her self-criticism and began to enjoy her classmates on a new level.

Every spring before the annual review for students in special education, we test them with the Woodcock-McGrew-Werder Mini-Battery of Achievement, an untimed and individually administered test, so that we can compare scores from year to year. Although this test has its limitations, Kristen's scores in reading went from a 3.2 to a 5.4 in fifth grade.

When reflecting on reading, listening, and speaking for her portfolio, Kristen said with confidence,

> First off, I would like to point out what I think are some of the most important things that I am able to do as a good reader. First, I think I have to understand the book to its fullest. Second, I think I have to relate to its characters. For example, in *Little House in the Big Woods*, I related to Laura best because she loved fall and animals.
>
> In a good book I feel that it must have lots of details. That's why I love the book *Number the Stars*. It was filled with descriptive details.
>
> My favorite type of reading is history but I can't really explain why. I'm just drawn to history books. Maybe it's because I enjoy seeing how people did things and how they were different.
>
> I think if I have a goal for next year it would be to be a better speaker. I would like to be able to place my words more carefully instead of just blurting them out. I would also like to be able to describe a book better. You see, when I try this task it seems I have a lot of pauses. I would like to fix that.
>
> I hope that I have helped you in understanding my year.

## What Students Say About Their Learning

At the end of each year, we ask the children to write a letter for their portfolio describing their learning. This letter is also a chance for them to introduce themselves to the teachers they will have the following year. These letters are self-edited, so teachers can see exactly what the children can do.

Jason, whose disability showed up mainly in writing, found his confidence when he began to write poetry. Early in the year, he wrote the poem about discovering a good book when the electricity went out (see Chapter 4). At the end of the year, he introduced himself to his next teacher as a poet (see Figure 46). Jason enjoys writing, thinks like a writer, and is realistic about his goals for next year. He knows what he needs to do but is not intimidated with his disabilities because he has received such positive support on his abilities.

Children become better readers by reading. Terrence (see Chapter 2) wrote with a sense of belonging to the learning community in his room (see Figure 47). He has stopped sitting with his back to the class or leaving the room in frustration. He has learned how to access information by listening and talking, and he likes to read in several genres.

---

### Figure 46
### Jason's Letter

Dear Fifth Grade Teacher,

I see my self as a poem writer: a writer determined to do the best I can in the best way I can. I write a lot of poems that talk about violence, about the fact that I'm a Jew and the holocaust. I write poems about my inspirations, my problems, the people I admire and the things every kid fears.

I think I have grown a lot this year. I think I have come to a higher understanding of poems and their inner meanings and how they apply to life. I have written great poems this year. Some of them really stand out. Because of that, I think I have become a stronger poet.

Poems have really grown on me. Every where I go, every thing I see gives me an idea of a poem. I hope I can continue writing them.

I like writing and my goals for next year are to improve my writing scores, hand writing and neatness. I do need improvement in areas like working on the computer and neatness and spelling. All in all I think I'm an ok writer but I want to be better.

---

### Figure 47
### Terrence's Letter

Dear, Sixed grade teacher,

Some of my stratgies for reading to understand words is to read it over and discusse a book with others.

Some of the things I did this year to become a better reader was to read out load so I can understand the words better, and I became better at finding the issues in books we read by listing to other peoples responses.

I became a better listener and speaker in book talk by understanding the book more and to lisen and not interouped people when they talk.

Some of the books I like to read is mysterrys, Action, monster and scary books ana biography books.

My goals for next year is to bee a faster reader.

What I look for in a good book is Action and adventure. I hate books that go on ana on and they get real boring

Remember Allyson, the child who wrote about a car trip (Chapter 3) and learned to love reading with Beverly Cleary taped books (Chapter 4)? Her letters to her fourth- and then fifth-grade teachers illustrate the progress that can occur in inclusive classrooms (see Figure 48). During third grade, her special education teacher pulled her out of the regular class for help. During fourth grade, she received the same amount of special education support (in time), but I worked with her in an inclusive classroom.

These students are right on target about what helps them learn and their goals for the future. Although test scores are only one measure of a child's success, all three of these students gained two or more years in their reading and writing scores during that school year. I do not believe their teachers and I worked magic—their success was an accumulation of many years of study and several teachers. However, I believe two factors made their scores jump so dramatically:

1. These students with disabilities felt empowered from the positive feedback they received from their two teachers and their peers, both general education and special education.

2. They especially benefited from having a balance of activities—lots of learning by listening and from seeing models and demonstrations of expectations—and time to practice reading and writing on their own.

## What Do Parents Say About Inclusive Classrooms?

Parents are a child's first and constant teacher. Their involvement and participation is essential for the success of any school program, whether it is general education, special education, or inclusive environments.

Many parents of children with disabilities are hesitant toward change. In previous years, they have had to recognize their child's disabilities and agree to a special education program, a change in the learning environment. Now they are being asked to look at the learning environment in yet another way. The most important assurance I can impart to them is that each child will receive as much support as he or she needs. With inclusion, we are not changing the amount of time a student receives support, but rather the setting. After all, special education is a service, not a place.

Michael's mother had serious reservations about the inclusion model. He had been eligible for resource room help in a pull-out model, which consisted of 45 minutes a day in a group of five students or less. She was knowledgeable about special education, both as a parent of a child with disabilities and as a teacher. She was not convinced that my working in the regular classroom for that amount of time would in any way be equal to the more individualized pull-out setting.

Michael's mother called me and came into school frequently to make sure that he was getting his required allotment of time daily. It was not too long before she

---

### Figure 48
### Allyson's Letters to Fourth- and Fifth-Grade Teachers

Dear 4th grade teacher

I like writing becaus
when you write you go
on all sots of adventur au
you imaggine yourself to be
there. You want the Reader
to get a picture in their
mind.
   I write about my life
because its fuin to writ
about. What I learnd about
writing to keep your hand
writing neat. And to use
descriptive langguage. And Ei
your workj!!!

---

Dear Fifth Grade Teacher,
   I can get ideas fast when I
write because, I have what I'm
going to put down next planned in my
head. The thing I like about
writing is. you get to keep your
memories, only on paper.
   Writing is another way of telling
your feelings. because, you write how
you feel about something, that you
don't want anybody to know about
I write in my room, because its
quiet and I can concentrate better
I write because it makes me
happy.
   My goals for the year are:
to write shorter sentences because,
sometimes one sentence can last a
paragraph. I also wont to write
longer paragraphs and to write
longer pieces.

began to see the difference in his attitude toward schoolwork and his increasing interest in reading and writing activities. I showed her drafts of his writing, where he was using more strategies as he worked. But she was still not convinced that he was getting enough skill and drill in the inclusion model.

However, by midyear, Michael's mother agreed that he was indeed getting the services specified on his IEP, and that he was changing and succeeding as a student in new ways. Michael felt like an integral part of the general education classroom, and he knew when he could work independently and when he needed assistance to meet grade level expectations.

I understand parents' concern when we change the delivery of services. When they are used to one format, there is a certain amount of anxiety in changing to another. Frequent communication with parents is always essential, but when we are providing assistance in new formats, such as inclusion or a balanced literacy approach, parents especially need to be kept informed.

Angela's mother and I often communicated by phone or in writing as we explored the line between student responsibility, teacher assistance, and home support in our effort to move Angela toward being a reflective, self-motivated learner in an inclusive classroom for the first time. At the beginning of the year, Angela never asked a question about any of her assignments, yet her homework was always perfectly done. During the fall, we noticed signs of anxiety and asked her mother to come in for a conference. We discovered that they were working together on homework every night and they were having arguments.

Once we had this background knowledge, we were able to change things on the spot. We all agreed that Angela would do her homework with her mother's encouragement but minimal assistance, and that if questions arose, Angela would bring them to the teachers at school. At first Angela was so reluctant to ask a question that her mother wrote me notes with the questions so the general education teacher and I knew what they were.

Angela discovered the legitimacy of having questions when she realized that other students in the class were asking questions all the time. She began to ask questions herself and participate in class discussions. Part of what I savored most was that she was becoming unafraid of not knowing, more willing to swirl in the unknown before the answer arrived.

Angela's mother and I continued to talk often. I urged her to let her child overcome obstacles with more independence. She respected this and tried, but in her heart she wanted to be helping more. She was unsure of the line between not helping enough and helping too much, between being there when needed and being there more than necessary. I can appreciate that concern; there is no exact answer.

In June I sent a questionnaire home to parents. Angela's mother apologized that she hurriedly scribbled answers to it, and yet she actually wrote with eloquence. It seems appropriate to end this book with her thoughts.

Q: When you first learned that your child would be receiving most of the special education services within the regular class, how did you feel?

A: *My first reaction was fear, then concern that she would not be able to feel the safety of the resource room, and if that were so, would she be able to focus and absorb the lesson. On the other hand, I was excited; this was the opportunity we have always wanted. Angela was very happy and my concerns vanished quickly. I guess you could say I had mixed feelings.*

Q: How do you help your child with homework?

A: *I do very little at this point. Of course it has not always been that way and I'm sure I will help her off and on in each new grade. I mostly ask Angela to check with her teachers if she has any real problems, in that way we don't have to battle over who is right or how it should be done.*

Q: Do you see a difference from September to June in how your child approaches school—time on task, taking responsibility, confidence...? Explain.

A: *Angela has become all of the above. I am certain that she has confidence. She is responsible and her approach is very positive. She started off on a rocket and has not landed yet!*

Q: Do you feel your child grew academically from having services provided in the general education class?

A: *Yes, yes, yes. Angela had role models, she learned through observation that even the best of students need help. I think all of this gave her confidence and allowed her potential to surface.*

Q: Do you feel your child has benefited socially from this type of service?

A: *I do feel the benefits were great in this setting. Angela is a shining example. Telling her that she was very much like the other children was not enough, she had to see this for herself. I think what I'd like to convey is my gratitude. Children are not basic, they are very complicated. They need, in their individual way, academic and emotional support. Every child is different yet their goal is to be the same. If you ask what it is that I am grateful for, I must say that all which has been offered to Angela in the past year (and longer than that) and all that is still to be offered, will one day give her the confidence to be different! Thank you for giving Angela the opportunity to be the same—for now.*

## SUGGESTED READING

Roller, C.M. (1996). *Variability not disability: Struggling readers in a workshop classroom*. Newark, DE: International Reading Association.

> This book is about working with students with disabilities from 8 to 12 years of age, and the importance of choice reading, formats for discussion, direct instruction, and record keeping.

Stires, S. (Ed.). (1991). *With promise: Redefining reading and writing for "special" students*. Portsmouth, NH: Heinemann.

> This is a compilation of the knowledge and thinking of many teacher-researchers and university researchers, looking at how we can redefine the way we teach reading and writing to students with special needs.

# Appendix

## Poetry Favorites for Read-Alouds

Alarcon, F.X. (1997). *Laughing tomatoes and other spring poems*. Ill. M.C. Gonzalez. San Francisco: Children's Book Press.

Asch, F. (1998). *Cactus poems*. Photog. T. Levin. Orlando, FL: Harcourt Brace.

Cullinan, B.E. (Ed.). (1996). *A jar of tiny stars: Poems by NCTE award-winning poets*. Honesdale, PA: Boyds Mills Press.

DeFina, A.A. (1997). *When a city leans against the sky*. Ill. K. Condon. Honesdale, PA: Boyds Mills Press.

Dotlich, R.K. (1998). *Lemonade sun and other summer poems*. Ill. J.S. Gilchrist. Honesdale, PA: Boyds Mills Press.

Fletcher, R. (1997). *Ordinary things: Poems from a walk in early spring*. Ill. W.L. Krudop. New York: Atheneum.

Florian, D. (1997). *In the swim*. Orlando, FL: Harcourt Brace.

George, K.O. (1998). *Old elm speaks: Tree poems*. Ill. K. Kiesler. New York: HarperCollins.

Greenfield, E. (1986). *Honey, I love and other poems*. Ill. L.D. Dillon & D. Dillon. New York: Harper Trophy.

Heard, G. (1997). *Creatures of earth, sea, and sky*. Ill. J.O. Dewey. Honesdale, PA: Boyds Mills Press.

Hopkins, L.B. (1993). *Extra innings*. Ill. S. Medlock. Orlando, FL: Harcourt Brace.

Livingston, M.C. (1986). *Earth songs*. New York: Scholastic.

Nye, N.S. (2000). *Come with me: Poems for a journey*. New York: Greenwillow.

Olaleye, I. (2001). *The distant talking drum: Poems from Nigeria*. Ill. F. Lessac. Honesdale, PA: Boyds Mills Press.

Spinelli, E. (1993). *If you want to find golden*. Ill. S. Schuett. Morton Grove, IL: Albert Whitman & Company.

Wong, J. (1996). *A suitcase of seaweed and other poems*. New York: Margaret K. McElderry.

Worth, V. (1994). *All the small poems and fourteen more*. Ill. N. Babbitt. New York: Farrar, Straus & Giroux.

## Picture Book Favorites for Read-Alouds

Baylor, B. (1986). *I'm in charge of celebrations*. Ill. P. Parnall. New York: Aladdin.

Bouchard, D. (1995). *If you're not from the prairie*. Ill. H. Ripplinger. New York: Aladdin.

Brown, M.W. (1999). *The important book*. Ill. L. Weisgard. New York: HarperCollins.

Buchholz, Q. (1999). *The collector of moments*. New York: Farrar, Straus & Giroux.

Bunting, E. (1996). *Going home*. Ill. D. Diaz. New York: HarperCollins.

Cherry, L. (1992). *A river ran wild*. Orlando, FL: Harcourt Brace.

Cooney, B. (1985). *Miss Rumphius*. New York: Viking.

Cowley, J. (1998). *Big moon tortilla*. Ill. D. Strongbow. Honesdale, PA: Boyds Mills Press.

Fletcher, R. (1997). *Twilight comes twice*. Ill. K. Kiesler. Boston: Houghton Mifflin.

Frasier, D. (1997). *On the day you were born*. Orlando, FL: Harcourt Brace.

Golenbock, P. (1992). *Teammates*. Ill. P. Bacon. Orlando, FL: Harcourt Brace.

Hendershot, J. (1992). *In coal country*. Ill. T.B. Allen. New York: Knopf.

High, L.O. (1999). *Barn savers*. Ill. T. Lewin. Honesdale, PA: Boyds Mills Press.

Hopkinson, D. (1995). *Sweet clara and the freedom quilt*. Ill. J. Ransome. New York: Random House.

Hucko, B. (1996). *A rainbow at night: The world in words and pictures by Navajo children*. San Francisco: Chronicle.

Jenkins, P. (1997). *A safe home for manatees*. Ill. M. Classen. New York: Harper Trophy.

Koch, M. (1993). *World water watch*. New York: Greenwillow.

Loewer, P., & Loewer, J. (1998). *The moonflower*. Atlanta, GA: Peachtree.

MacLachlan, P. (1983). *Through grandpa's eyes*. Ill. D.K. Ray. New York: Harper Trophy.

Martin, B., Jr., & Archambault, J. (1983). *Knots on a counting rope*. Ill. T. Rand. New York: Harper Trophy.

Martin, J.B. (1998). *Snowflake bentley*. Ill. M. Azarian. Boston: Houghton Mifflin.

Mitchell, M.K. (1998). *Uncle Jed's barbershop*. Ill. J. Ransome. New York: Aladdin.

Nolen, J. (2001). *In my momma's kitchen*. Ill. C. Bootman. New York: Harper Trophy.

Polacco, P. (2001). *The keeping quilt*. New York: Aladdin.

Ringgold, F. (1996). *Tar Beach*. New York: Dragonfly.

Rylant, C. (1991). *Night in the country*. Ill. M. Szilagyi. New York: Aladdin.

Rylant, C. (1999). *An angel for Solomon Singer*. Ill. P. Catalanotto. Topeka, KS: Econo-Clad Books.

Rylant, C. (2001). *The relatives came*. Ill. S. Gammell. New York: Atheneum.

Say, A. (1993). *Grandfather's journey*. Boston: Houghton Mifflin.

Shea, P.D. (1999). *The whispering cloth*. Topeka, KS: Econo-Clad Books.

Van Allsburg, C. (1990). *Just a dream*. Boston: Houghton Mifflin.

Waldman, N. (1999). *The starry night*. Honesdale, PA: Boyds Mills Press.

Williams, V.B. (1984). *A chair for my mother*. New York: Greenwillow.

Wright-Frierson, V. (1996). *A desert scrapbook: Dawn to dusk in the Sonora*. New York: Simon & Schuster.

Yolen, J. (1987). *Owl moon*. Ill. J. Schoenherr. New York: Philomel.

Yolen, J. (1997). *Welcome to the green house*. Ill. L. Regan. New York: Putnam.

Zolotow, C. (1994). *The seashore book*. Ill. W. Minor. New York: Harper Trophy.

## Short Stories for Read-Alouds and Independent Reading

Carle, E. (1997). *Flora and Tiger: 19 very short stories from my life*. New York: Philomel.

Cisneros, S. (1994). *The house on Mango Street*. New York: Knopf.

Fleischman, P. (1999). *Seedfolks*. New York: Harper Trophy.

Little, J. (1990). *Hey world, here I am!* Ill. S. Truesdell. New York: Harper Trophy.

Myers, W.D. (2000). *145th Street: Short stories*. New York: Delacorte.

Shannon, G. (2001). *More stories to solve: Fifteen folktales from around the world*. Ill. P. Sis. New York: Harper Trophy.

## Read-Alouds and the Westward Movement

Anderson, J. (1985). *Christmas on the prairie*. New York: Clarion.

Anderson, J. (1987). *Joshua's westward journal*. New York: William Morrow.

Anderson, J. (1999). *Pioneer children of Appalachia*. Topeka, KS: Econo-Clad Books.

Benet, R., & Benet, S.V. (1999). Western wagon. In N. Panzer (Ed.), *Celebrate America in poetry and art*. New York: Hyperion Press.

Erickson, P. (1997). *Daily life in a covered wagon*. New York: Puffin.

Freedman, R. (1995). *Buffalo hunt*. New York: Holiday House.

Freedman, R. (1999). *Cowboys of the Wild West*. Topeka, KS: Econo-Clad Books.

Harness, C. (1999). *The amazing impossible Erie Canal*. New York: Aladdin.

Kalman, B. (1992). *Tools and gadgets: Historic communities*. New York: Crabtree Publishers.

Kroll, S. (1996). *Lewis and Clark. Explorers of the American West*. Ill. R. Williams. New York: Holiday House.

Kurelek, W. (1999). *A prairie boy's winter*. Topeka, KS: Econo-Clad Books.

Levine, E. (1992). *If you traveled West in a covered wagon*. Ill. E. Freem. New York: Scholastic.

Rounds, G. (1996). *Sod houses on the Great Plains*. New York: Holiday House.

Turner, A. (1997). *Mississippi mud: Three prairie journals*. Ill. R. Blake. New York: HarperCollins.

Van Leeuwen, J. (1992). *Going West*. New York: Dial.

## Books for a Memoir Study

Brinckloe, J. (1985). *Fireflies!* New York: Aladdin.

Bunting, E. (1996). *Going home*. Ill. D. Diaz. New York: Harper Trophy.

Byars, B. (1996). *The moon and I*. New York: Beach Tree.

Carle, E. (1997). *Flora and Tiger: 19 very short stories from my life*. New York: Philomel.

Cisneros, S. (1994). *The house on Mango Street*. New York: Knopf.

Crews, D. (1998). *Bigmama's*. New York: Mulberry.

Garza, C.L. (1996). *In my family: En mi Familia*. San Francisco: Children's Book Press.

Graves, D. (1996). *Baseball, snakes and summer squash*. Honesdale, PA: Boyds Mills Press.

Gray, L.M. (1999). *My mama had a dancing heart*. Danbury, CT: Orchard Books.

Greenfield, E., & Little, L.J. (1993). *Childtimes*. New York: HarperCollins.

Gunning, M. (1999). *Not a copper penny in me house: Poems from the Carribbean*. Ill. F. Lessac. Honesdale, PA: Boyds Mills Press.

Herrera, J.F. (1995). *Calling the doves*. Ill. E. Simmons. San Francisco: Children's Book Press.

Hest, A. (1995). *How to get famous in Brooklyn*. Ill. L.D. Sawaya. New York: Simon & Schuster.

Hopkins, L.B. (1999). *Been to yesterdays*. Honesdale, PA: Boyds Mills Press.

MacLachlan, P. (1994). *All the places to love*. Ill. M. Wimmer. New York: HarperCollins.

Medina, J. (1999). *My name is Jorge*. Ill. F.V. Broeck. Honesdale, PA: Boyds Mills Press.

Nickens, B. (1994). *Walking the Log: Memories of a Southern childhood*. New York: Rizzoli.

Nolen, J. (2001). *In my momma's kitchen*. Ill. C. Bootman. New York: Harper Trophy.

Polacco, P. (1989). *Uncle Vova's tree*. New York: Philomel.

Polacco, P. (1995). *Babushka's doll*. New York: Aladdin.

Polacco, P. (1998). *Thank you, Mr. Falker*. New York: Philomel.

Say, A. (1993). *Grandfather's journey*. Boston: Houghton Mifflin.

Soto, G. (1992). *Neighborhood odes*. Orlando, FL: Harcourt Brace.

Wong, J.S. (1996). *A suitcase of seaweed*. New York: Margaret K. McElderry.

## Popular Series

Aldo Applesauce, Johanna Hurwitz
Amber Brown, Paula Danziger

Amelia Bedelia, Peggy Parrish
American Girls Collection
Anastasia, Lois Lowry
Anne of Green Gables, L.M. Montgomery
Arthur, Lillian Hoban
Arthur, Marc Brown
Bingo Brown, Betsy Byars
Bunnicula, James Howe
Cam Jansen Adventures, David A. Adler
The Chronicles of Narnia, C.S. Lewis
Commander Toad, Jane Yolen
Curious George, H.A. Rey
Einstein Anderson Science Detective, Seymour Simon
Encyclopedia Brown, Donald J. Sobol
Fox, James Marshall
Frances, Russell Hoban
Frog and Toad, Arnold Lobel
George and Martha, J. Marshall
The Great Brain, John D. Fitzgerald
Harry Potter, J.K. Rowling
Henry and Mudge, Cynthia Rylant
Henry Huggins, Beverly Cleary
Jigsaw Jones Mysteries, James Preller
Julian and Huey, Ann Cameron
Little Bear, Else Homelund Minarik
Little House on the Prairie, Laura Ingles Wilder
The Littles, John Peterson
Miss Nelson Series, Harry Allard and James Marshall
Mr. Putter and Tabby, Cynthia Rylant
Nate the Great, Marjorie Weinman Sharmat
One Day, Jean Craighead George
Paddington Bear, Michael Bond
Pippi Longstocking, Astrid Lindgren
Polk Street School Series, Patricia Reilly Giff
Poppleton, Cynthia Rylant
Ramona, Beverly Cleary
Sports Series, Matt Christopher
Time Warp, Jon Scieszka

# Nonfiction to Interest Struggling Readers

## *Picture Books*

Baylor, B. (1984). *If you are a hunter of fossils*. Ill. P. Parnall. New York: Aladdin.
Bunting, E. (1997). *I am the mummy Heb-Nefert*. Ill. D. Christiana. San Diego: Harcourt Brace.
Bunting, E. (1998). *So far from the sea*. Ill. C. Soentpiet. New York: Clarion.
Bunting, E. (1999). *Butterfly house*. Ill. G. Shed. New York: Scholastic.

Cherry, L. (1992). *A river ran wild*. San Diego: Harcourt Brace.

Cone, M. (1992). *Come back, salmon: How a group of dedicated kids adopted Pigeon Creek and brought it back to life*. Ill. S. Wheelwright. New York: Sierra Club.

Cooper, F. (1994). *Coming home: From the life of Langston Hughes*. New York: Philomel.

Cummings, P. (1992). *Talking with artists*. New York: Bradbury.

Dewey, J.O. (1997). *Rattlesnake dance: True tales, mysteries, and rattlesnake ceremonies*. Honesdale, PA: Boyds Mills Press.

Duggleby, J. (1998). *Story painter: The life of Jacob Lawrence*. San Francisco: Chronicle.

Florian, D. (2000). *Mammalabilia: Poems and paintings*. San Diego: Harcourt Brace.

Frasier, D. (1991). *On the day you were born*. San Diego: Harcourt Brace.

Frasier, D. (1998). *Out of the ocean*. San Diego: Harcourt Brace.

Freedman, R. (1987). *Lincoln: A photobiography*. New York: Clarion.

Freedman, R. (1997). *Out of darkness: The story of Louis Braille*. Ill. K. Kiesler. New York: Clarion.

George, J.C. (1995). *Everglades*. Ill. W. Minor. New York: HarperCollins.

George, J.C. (1996). *The tarantula in my purse and 172 other wild pets*. New York: HarperCollins.

Golenbock, P. (1990). *Teammates*. Ill. P. Bacon. Orlando, FL: Harcourt Brace.

Holzer, H. (Ed.). (2000). *Abraham Lincoln: The writer*. Honesdale, PA: Boyds Mills Press.

Hucko, B. (1996). *A rainbow at night: The world in words and pictures by Navajo children*. San Francisco: Chronicle.

Jones, C. (1996). *Accidents may happen: Fifty inventions discovered by mistake*. Ill. J. O'Brien. New York: Delacorte.

Knight, M.B. (1992). *Talking walls*. Ill. A. O'Brien. Gardiner, ME: Tibury House.

Kroll, S. (1994). *Lewis and Clark: Explorers of the American West*. New York: Holiday House.

Lourie, P. (1992). *Hudson River: An adventure from the mountains to the sea*. Honesdale, PA: Boyds Mills Press.

Martin, J.B. (1998). *Snowflake Bentley*. Ill. M. Azarian. Boston: Houghton Mifflin.

McMahon, P. (1993). *Chi-Hoon: A Korean girl*. Ill. M. O'Brien. Honesdale, PA: Boyds Mills Press.

Miller, W. (1994). *Zora Hurston and the chinaberry tree*. Illus. C. VanWright & Y. Hu. New York: Lee and Low.

Myers, J. (2001). *How dogs came from wolves and other explorations of science in action*. Honesdale, PA: Boyds Mills Press.

Pinkney, A. (1993). *Alvin Ailey*. Ill. B. Pinkney. New York: Hyperion.

Pratt, K.J. (1992). *A walk in the rainforest*. Nevada City, CA: Dawn.

Pratt, K.J. (1994). *A swim through the sea*. Nevada City, CA: Dawn.

Pratt, K.J. (1996). *A fly in the sky*. Nevada City, CA: Dawn.

Simon, S. (1989). *Whales*. New York: Scholastic.

Stafford, K. (1994). *We got here together*. Ill. D. Frasier. San Diego: Harcourt Brace.

Swinburne, S. (1999). *Coyote: North America's dog*. Honesdale, PA: Boyds Mills Press.

## Nonfiction Books for Guided and Independent Reading

All-Pro Biographies, Children's Press (Examples: Joe Dumars, Florence Griffith-Joyner)

Eyewitness Juniors, Knopf (Random House) (Example: *Amazing Crocodiles and Reptiles*)

Kids Discover (Examples: Each issue focuses on a key theme such as Lewis and Clark, Ancient Greece, Energy)

Little Celebrations, Celebration Press (HarperCollins) (Examples: Tiger Tales, Whales, Little Critter Journal)

National Geographic Reading Expeditions (Examples: The Southwest, Colonial Life, Egypt, An Immigrant Community of the 1900s)

Newbridge nonfiction leveled books (Examples: Rain Forest, Matter, Wild Weather, Can Kids Save the Earth?)

Orbit Chapter books from Pacific Learning (Examples: Searching for Sea Lions, Creatures of the Reef, Canoe Diary, The Shapes of Water)

Pair-It Books (pairing fiction and nonfiction), Steck-Vaughn (Examples: Diary of a Pioneer Boy/The Pioneer Way, The Mystery of the Missing Leopard/Wild Cats, Facing the Flood/Nature's Power, The Art Riddle Contest/Artists and Their Art)

Rookie Biographies, Children's Press (Examples: Martin Luther King, George Washington, John Muir)

Zoobooks, Wildlife Education (Example: Each issue focuses on a single animal or group of animals such as Birds of Prey.)

## *Magazines*

*Cricket*
*Faces: People, Places and Culture* (Cobblestone Publishing)
*National Geographic for Kids*
*Ranger Rick* (National Wildlife Federation)
*Sports Illustrated for Kids*
*Time for Kids*
*World Magazine* (National Geographic Society)

# Books That Pair Art With Poetry

Angelou, M. (1987). *Now Sheba sings the song*. Ill. T. Feelings. New York: Dutton.

Brenner, B. (Ed.). (2000). *Voices: Poetry and art from around the world*. Washington, DC: National Geographic Society.

Burleigh, R. (1997). *Hoops*. Ill. S.T. Johnson. San Diego: Harcourt Brace.

Fox, D. (Ed.) (1987). *Go in and out the window: An illustrated songbook for young people*. New York: The Metropolitan Museum of Art/Henry Holt.

Frost, R. (1985). *Stopping by woods on a snowy evening*. Ill. S. Jeffers. New York: Dutton.

Frost, R. (1990). *Birches*. Ill. E. Young. New York: Henry Holt.

Greenberg, J. (Ed.). (2001). *Heart to heart: New poems inspired by twentieth-century American art*. New York: Harry N. Abrams.

Hines, A.G. (2001). *Pieces: A year in poems and quilts*. New York: Greenwillow.

Hopkins, L.B. (Ed.). (1997). *Marvelous math: A book of poems*. Ill. K. Barbour. New York: Simon & Schuster.

Hopkins, L.B. (Ed.). (2000). *My America: A poetry atlas of the United States*. Ill. S. Alcorn. New York: Simon & Schuster.

Hughes, L. (1995). *The block: Poems*. Ill. R. Bearden. New York: The Metropolitan Museum of Art/Viking.

Koch, K., & Farrell, K. (1985). *Talking to the sun: An illustrated anthology of poems for young people*. New York: Henry Holt.

Locker, T. (1997). *Water dance*. San Diego: Harcourt Brace.

Myers, W.D. (1997). *Harlem*. Ill. C. Myers. New York: Scholastic.

Nye, N.S. (Ed.). (1998). *The space between our footsteps: Poems and paintings from the Middle East*. New York: Simon & Schuster.

Panzer, N. (Ed.). (1999). *Celebrate America: In poetry and art*. New York: Hyperion.

Shange, N. (1994). *I live in music*. Ill. R. Bearden. New York: Welcome Books.

Sullivan, C. (Ed.). (1991). *Children of promise: African-American literature and art for young people*. New York: Harry N. Abrams.

Whipple, L. (1994). *Celebrating America: A collection of poems and images of the American spirit*. New York: Philomel.

Yolen, J. (1995). *Water music: Poems for children*. Photog. J. Stemple. Honesdale, PA: Boyds Mills Press.

Yolen, J. (1996). *Sacred places*. Ill. D. Shannon. San Diego: Harcourt Brace.

# References

Allington, R.L. (2001). *What really matters for struggling readers: Designing research-based programs*. New York: Longman.

Allington, R.L., & Cunningham, P.M. (1996). *Schools that work: Where all children read and write*. Reading, MA: Addison-Wesley.

Anderson, R.C., Hiebert, E.H., Scott, J.A., & Wilkinson, I.A.G. (1985). *Becoming a nation of readers: The report of the Commission on Reading*. Washington, DC: National Institute of Education.

Anderson, R.C., Wilson, P.T., & Fielding, L.G. (1988). Growth in reading and how children spend their time outside of school. *Reading Research Quarterly, 23*, 285–303.

Atwell, N. (Ed.). (1990). *Coming to know: Writing to learn in the intermediate grades*. Portsmouth, NH: Heinemann.

Au, K.H., Carroll, J.H., & Scheu, J.A. (2001). *Balanced literacy instruction* (2nd ed.). Norwood, MA: Christopher-Gordon.

Barton, B. (2000). *Telling stories your way: Storytelling and reading aloud in the classroom*. York, ME: Stenhouse.

Calkins, L. (2001). *The art of teaching reading*. New York: Longman.

Cambourne, B. (1995). Toward an educationally relevant theory of literacy learning: Twenty years of inquiry. *The Reading Teacher, 49*, 182–190.

Chall, J.S., & Conrad, S.S. (1991). *Should textbooks challenge students?* New York: Teachers College Press.

Cipielewski, J., & Stanovich, K. (1992). Predicting growth in reading ability from children's exposure to print. *Journal of Experimental Child Psychology, 54*, 74–89.

Clay, M. (1993). *An observation survey of early literacy achievement*. Portsmouth, NH: Heinemann.

Clay, M. (1998). *By different paths to common outcomes*. York, ME: Stenhouse.

Cooper, J.D. (1997). *Literacy: Helping children construct meaning*. Boston: Houghton Mifflin.

Corgill, A. (1999, April). Ruminations on a lingering question. *Primary Voices K–6, 7*(4), 39.

Cullinan, B.E. (2000). *Let's read about: Finding books they'll love to read* (2nd ed.). New York: Scholastic.

Cullinan, B.E., Scala, M.C., & Schroder, V.C. (1995). *Three voices: An invitation to poetry across the curriculum*. York, ME: Stenhouse.

Daniels, H. (1994). *Literature circles: Voice and choice in the student-centered classroom*. York, ME: Stenhouse.

Daniels, H. (2001). *Looking into literature circles* [Video]. York, ME: Stenhouse.

Donahue, P.L., Voelkl, K.E., Campbell, J.R., & Mazzeo, J. (1999). *NAEP 1998 reading report card for the nation and the states*. Washington, DC: National Center for Education Statistics.

Duffy-Hester, A. (1999). Teaching struggling readers in elementary school classrooms: A review of classroom reading programs and principles for instruction. *The Reading Teacher, 52*, 490–495.

Elbaum, B., Schumm, J.S., & Vaughn, S. (1997). Urban middle-elementary students' perceptions of grouping formats for reading instruction. *The Elementary School Journal, 97*(5), 475–500.

Elley, W.B. (1992). *How in the world do students read?* IEA Study of Reading Literacy. The Hague, Netherlands: International Association for the Evaluation of Educational Achievement.

Fletcher, R.J. (1993). *What a writer needs*. Portsmouth, NH: Heinemann.

Fletcher, R.J. (1996). *Breathing in, breathing out: Keeping a writer's notebook*. Portsmouth, NH: Heinemann.

Foertsch, M. (1992). *Reading in and out of school*. Princeton, NJ: Educational Testing Service.

Fountas, I.C., & Pinnell, G.S. (2001). *Guiding readers and writers grades 3–6: Teaching comprehension, genre, and content literacy*. Portsmouth, NH: Heinemann.

Galda, L., & Cullinan, B.E. (2002). *Literature and the child* (5th ed.). Belmont, CA: Wadsworth.

Goodman, K.S. (1969). Analysis of oral reading miscues: Applied psycholinguistics. *Reading Research Quarterly, 5*, 9–30.

Goodman, Y.M. (1978). Kidwatching: An alternative to testing. *National Elementary School Principal, 57*, 41–45.

Graves, M.F., & Graves, B.B. (1994). *Scaffolding reading experiences: Designs for student success*. Norwood, MA: Christopher-Gordon.

Greene, R.W. (2001). *The explosive child: A new approach for understanding and parenting easily frustrated, chronically inflexible children*. New York: HarperCollins.

Hart-Hewins, L., & Wells, J. (1999). *Better books! Better readers! How to choose, use and level books for children in the primary grades*. York, ME: Stenhouse.

Harvey, S. (1998). *Nonfiction matters: Reading, writing, and research in grades 3–8*. York, ME: Stenhouse.

Harvey, S., & Goudvis, A. (2000). *Strategies that work: Teaching comprehension to enhance understanding*. York, ME: Stenhouse.

Holdaway, D. (1979). *The foundations of literacy*. Portsmouth, NH: Heinemann.

Isaacson, S.L. (1992). Volleyball and other analogies: A response to Englert. *Journal of Learning Disabilities, 25*(3), 173–177.

Keefe, C.H. (1996). *Label-free learning: Supporting learners with disabilities*. York, ME: Stenhouse.

Keene, E.O., & Zimmermann, S. (1997). *Mosaic of thought: Teaching comprehension in a reader's workshop*. Portsmouth, NH: Heinemann.

Koefoed, B. (2000). *An observation survey: The video*. Portsmouth, NH: Heinemann.

Krashen, S. (1996). *Every person a reader*. Culver City, CA: Language Education Associates.

McBride-Chang, C., Manis, F., Seidenberg, M., Custodio, R., & Doi, L. (1993). Print exposure as a predictor of word reading and reading comprehension in disabled and nondisabled readers. *Journal of Educational Psychology, 85*, 230–238.

Mooney, M. (1995). Guided reading beyond the primary grades. *Teaching Pre-K–8, 26*(1), 75–77.

Nagy, W., Herman, P., & Anderson, R. (1985). Learning words from context. *Reading Research Quarterly, 20*, 233–253.

New Zealand Ministry of Education. (1997). *Reading for life: The learner as a reader*. Katonah, NY: Richard C. Owen.

Nia, I. (1998, April). Story matters. *The Council Chronicle*, p. 14.

Northern Nevada Writing Project Teacher-Reader Group. (1996). *Team teaching*. York, ME: Stenhouse.

Nye, N.S. (1994). *Red suitcase*. Brockport, NY: BOA Editions.

Opitz, M. (1998). *Flexible grouping in reading: Practical ways to help all students become stronger readers*. New York: Scholastic.

Parker, D. (1997). *Jamie: A literacy story*. York, ME: Stenhouse.

Parkes, B. (2000). *Read it again! Revisiting shared reading.* York, ME: Stenhouse.

Pikulski, J.J. (1994). Preventing reading failure: A review of five effective programs. *The Reading Teacher, 48,* 30–39.

Pume, M.J., Karweit, N., Price, C., Ricciuti, A., Thompson, W., & Vaden-Kiernan, M. (1997). *Prospects: Final report on student outcomes.* Washington, DC: U.S. Department of Education, Planning and Evaluation.

Rhodes, L.K., & Dudley-Marling, C. (1988). *Readers and writers with a difference: A holistic approach to teaching learning disabled and remedial students.* Portsmouth, NH: Heinemann.

Roberts, S. (2000, April 27). After trading hits, the raptors fall. *The New York Times,* p. D-1.

Roberts, S. (2000, September 3). Gambill plays it cool to hold off Philippoussis. *The New York Times,* p. D-1.

Routman, R. (2000). *Conversations: Strategies for teaching, learning, and evaluating.* Portsmouth, NH: Heinemann.

Scala, M.A. (1998, March/April). Is inclusion working in your school? *Creative Classroom,* p. 29.

Segel, E. (1986). *Short takes: A short story collection for young readers* (p. vii). New York: Dell.

Snowball, D. (2000). *Focus on spelling* [Inservice Video Series]. York, ME: Stenhouse.

Snowball, D., & Bolton, F. (1999). *Spelling K–8: Planning and teaching.* York, ME: Stenhouse.

Syzmusiak, K., & Sibberson, F. (2001). *Beyond leveled books: Supporting transitional readers in grades 2–5.* York, ME: Stenhouse.

Taberski, S. (2000). *On solid ground: Strategies for teaching reading K–3.* Portsmouth, NH: Heinemann.

Toussaint, P. (1999). *Great books for African-American children.* New York: Penguin.

Trelease, J. (1995). *The read-aloud handbook* (4th ed.). New York: Penguin.

Trousdale, A.M. (1990). Interactive storytelling: Scaffolding children's early narratives. *Language Arts, 67,* 173.

Wooten, D.A. (2000). *Valued voices: An interdisciplinary approach to teaching and learning.* Newark, DE: International Reading Association.

# Children's Literature Cited

Alarcon, F.X. (1997). *Laughing tomatoes and other spring poems.* Ill. M.C. Gonzalez. San Francisco: Children's Book Press.

Armstrong, W.H. (1969). *Sounder.* New York: Harper Trophy.

Asch, F. (1996). *Sawgrass poems: A view of the Everglades.* Photog. T. Levin. Orlando, FL: Harcourt Brace.

Asch, F. (1998). *Cactus poems.* Photog. T. Levin. Orlando, FL: Harcourt Brace.

Baron, V. (Ed.) (1968). *The seasons of time: Tanka poetry of ancient Japan.* New York: Dial.

Baron, V. (Ed.) (1974). *Sunset in a spider web: Sijo poetry of ancient Korea.* New York: Holt, Rinehart and Winston.

Baylor, B. (1986). *I'm in charge of celebrations.* New York: Charles Scribner's Sons.

Bolton, F. (1996). *The greedy goat.* Greenvale, NY: Mondo Publishers.

Briggs, R. (1987). *The Snowman.* New York: Random House.

Bunting, E. (1996). *Going home.* New York: HarperCollins.

Byars, B.C. (1970). *The summer of the swans.* Ill. T. Coconis. New York: Viking.

Byars, B.C. (1993). *The pinballs.* New York: HarperCollins.

Byars, B.C. (1996). *The midnight fox.* Ill. A. Grifalconi. New York: Viking.

Byars, B.C. (1996). *The moon and I*. New York: Beech Tree Books.

Choi, S.N. (1993). *Halmoni and the picnic*. Ill. K.M. Dugan. Boston: Houghton Mifflin.

Cleary, B. (1991). *Muggy Maggie*. New York: Camelot.

Collier, J.L., & Collier, C. (1989). *My brother Sam is dead*. New York: Scholastic.

Cone, M. (1994). *Come back, salmon: How a group of dedicated kids adopted Pigeon Creek and brought it back to life*. Photog. S. Wheelwright. San Francisco: Sierra Club Books.

Conrad, P. (1991). *My Daniel*. New York: HarperCollins.

De Fina, A.A. (1997). "Riding the subway train." *When a city leans against the sky: Poems*. Ill. K. Condon. Honesdale, PA: Boyds Mills Press.

Dotlich, R. (1998). *Lemonade Sun and other summer poems*. Honesdale, PA: Boyds Mills Press.

Facklam, M. (1993). *And then there was one: The mysteries of extinction*. Boston: Little, Brown.

Fletcher, R.J. (1996). *A writer's notebook: Unlocking the writer within you*. New York: Camelot.

Fletcher, R.J. (1997). *Twilight comes twice*. Ill. K. Kiesler. Boston: Houghton Mifflin.

Florian, D. (1998). *Insectlopedia*. New York: Harcourt Brace.

Fritz, J. (1987). *The cabin faced West*. Ill. F. Rojankovsky. New York: Viking Press.

Fritz, J. (1998). *Shh! We're writing the Constitution*. Ill. T. dePaola. New York: Paper Star.

George, J.C. (2000). *My side of the mountain*. New York: Penguin.

George, K.O. (1998). *Old elm speaks: Tree poems*. Ill. K. Kiesler. Boston: Houghton Mifflin.

Giovanni, N. (1987). *Spin a soft black song*. Ill. G. Martins. New York: Hill and Wang.

Graves, D. (1996). *Baseball, snakes, and summer squash: Poems about growing up*. Honesdale, PA: Boyds Mills Press.

Heard, G. (1997). *Creatures of earth, sea, and sky*. Honesdale, PA: Boyds Mills Press.

Herrera, J.F. (1995). *Calling the doves*. Ill. E. Simmons. San Francisco: Children's Book Press.

Hesse, K. (1999). *Out of the dust*. New York: Scholastic.

Hopkinson, D. (1995). *Sweet Clara and the freedom quilt*. Ill. J. Ransome. New York: Random House.

Hughes, L. (1996). *The Dream Keeper and other poems*. Ill. B. Pinkney. New York: Knopf.

James, S. (1996). *Meet the octopus*. Greenvale, NY: Mondo.

Keegan, M. (1993). *Mother Earth Father Sky: Pueblo and Navajo Indians of the Southwest*. Santa Fe, NM: Clear Light Publishers.

Krensky, S. (1999). *King Arthur*. Boston: Little, Brown.

Lawlor, V. (1997). *I was dreaming to come to America: Memories from the Ellis Island oral history project*. New York: Puffin.

Lewis, C.S. (1994). *The lion, the witch, and the wardrobe* (The Chronicles of Narnia, Book 2). New York: HarperCollins.

Lord, B.B. (1986). *In the year of the boar and Jackie Robinson*. New York: Harper Trophy.

Lowry, L. (1994). *The giver*. New York: Bantam.

Lowry, L. (1998). *Number the stars*. New York: Laureleaf.

MacLachlan, P. (1993). *Journey*. New York: Dell Yearling.

MacLachlan, P. (1994). *All the places to love*. Ill. M. Wimmer. New York: HarperCollins.

Mayer, M. (1992). *A boy, a dog, and a frog*. New York: Dial.

McGovern, A. (1978). *Shark Lady*. New York: Scholastic.

Medina, J. (1999). *My name is Jorge: On both sides of the river*. Ill. F.V. Broeck. Honesdale, PA: Boyds Mills Press.

Mohr, N. (1999). *Felita*. New York: Puffin.

Moss, J. (1989). *The butterfly jar*. New York: Bantam Books for Young Readers.

Owens, T.S. (1998). *Ellis Island* (The Library of American Landmarks). Logan, IA: Powerkids Press.

Rylant, C. (1988). *Every living thing.* Ill. S.D. Schindler. New York: Aladdin.

Rylant, C. (1997). *Henry and Mudge and the careful cousin.* New York: Aladdin.

Say, A. (1993). *Grandfather's journey.* Boston: Houghton Mifflin.

Shea, P.D. (1996). *The whispering cloth: A refugee's story.* Honesdale, PA: Boyds Mills Press.

Silverstein, S. (1981). "Ation." *A light in the attic.* New York: HarperCollins.

Spier, P. (1986). *Dreams.* New York: Doubleday.

Spier, P. (1997). *Rain.* New York: Dell Yearling.

Spier, P. (1999). *We the people: The Constitution of the United States.* Topeka, KS: Econo-Clad.

Spinelli, J. (1998). *Wringer.* New York: Harper Trophy.

Steig, W. (1992). *Amos & Boris.* New York: Sunburst Books.

Strickland, D.S., & Strickland, M.R. (Eds.). (1994). *Families: Poems celebrating the African American experience.* Ill. J. Ward. Honesdale, PA: Boyds Mills Press.

Taylor, T. (1991). *The cay.* New York: Avon.

Turner, A. (1989). *Dakota Dugout.* Ill. R. Himler. New York: Aladdin.

Van Allsburg, C. (1982). *Ben's dream.* Boston: Houghton Mifflin.

Wiesner, D. (1991). *Tuesday.* New York: Clarion.

Wiesner, D. (1999). *Sector 7.* Boston: Houghton Mifflin.

# Index

Note: Page numbers followed by *f* indicate figures.